Political Translation

At a time when the legitimacy of democracies is in question, calls to improve the quality of public debate and deliberative democracy are sweeping the social sciences. Yet, real deliberation lies far from the deliberative ideal. Theorists have argued that linguistic and cultural differences foster inequality and impede democratic deliberation. In this empirical study, the author presents the collective practices of *political translation*, which help multilingual and culturally diverse groups work together more democratically than do homogeneous groups. *Political translation*, distinct from linguistic translation, is a set of disruptive and communicative practices developed by activists and grassroots community organizers to address inequities hindering democratic deliberation and entreat powerful groups to work together more inclusively with disempowered groups. Based on almost ten years of fieldwork, *Political Translation* provides the first systematic comparative study of deliberation under conditions of linguistic difference and cultural misunderstandings.

Nicole Doerr is Associate Professor of Sociology at the University of Copenhagen. Doerr's research investigates how and under what conditions increased linguistic and cultural diversity fosters democratic innovation in the areas of social movements, local democracy, and participation by migrants, refugees, and minorities. Based on research in the United States, Germany, Italy, South Africa, and the United Kingdom, Doerr explores the collective practices of political translation, which can help multilingual and diverse groups work together more democratically and foster intersectional gendered inclusion. Doerr's research has been awarded the EU Marie Curie and IPODI Fellowships, as well as the Harvard Ash Center Democracy Fellowship.

Cambridge Studies in Contentious Politics

General Editor

Doug McAdam *Stanford University and Center for Advanced Study in the Behavioral Sciences*

Editors

Mark Beissinger *Princeton University*
Donatella della Porta *Scuola Normale Superiore*
Jack A. Goldstone *George Mason University*
Michael Hanagan *Vassar College*
Holly J. McCammon *Vanderbilt University*
David S. Meyer *University of California, Irvine*
Sarah Soule *Stanford University*
Suzanne Staggenborg *University of Pittsburgh*
Sidney Tarrow *Cornell University*
Charles Tilly (d. 2008) *Columbia University*
Elisabeth J. Wood *Yale University*
Deborah Yashar *Princeton University*

(continued after index)

Political Translation

How Social Movement Democracies Survive

NICOLE DOERR

University of Copenhagen

CAMBRIDGE
UNIVERSITY PRESS

CAMBRIDGE
UNIVERSITY PRESS

University Printing House, Cambridge CB2 8BS, United Kingdom

One Liberty Plaza, 20th Floor, New York, NY 10006, USA

477 Williamstown Road, Port Melbourne, VIC 3207, Australia

314–321, 3rd Floor, Plot 3, Splendor Forum, Jasola District Centre, New Delhi – 110025, India

79 Anson Road, #06–04/06, Singapore 079906

Cambridge University Press is part of the University of Cambridge.

It furthers the University's mission by disseminating knowledge in the pursuit of education, learning, and research at the highest international levels of excellence.

www.cambridge.org
Information on this title: www.cambridge.org/9781108420716
DOI: 10.1017/9781108355087

First published 2018

Printed in the United Kingdom by Clays, St Ives plc

A catalogue record for this publication is available from the British Library.

Library of Congress Cataloging-in-Publication Data
NAMES: Doerr, Nicole, author.
TITLE: Political translation : how social movement democracies survive / Nicole Doerr.
DESCRIPTION: New York : Cambridge University Press, 2018. | Series: Cambridge studies in contentious politics | Includes bibliographical references and index.
IDENTIFIERS: LCCN 2017053336| ISBN 9781108420716 (hardback) | ISBN 9781108430791 (paperback)
SUBJECTS: LCSH: Multiculturalism. | Democracy. | Social movements.
CLASSIFICATION: LCC HM1271 .D64 2018 | DDC 303.48/4–dc23
LC record available at https://lccn.loc.gov/2017053336

ISBN 978-1-108-42071-6 Hardback
ISBN 978-1-108-43079-1 Paperback

Contents

Tables

Acknowledgments

For their generosity over the course of this long-term ethnographic research project, I am deeply indebted to the nearly 150 activists, community organizers, and Social Forum organizers in Europe, Turkey, and the United States who took time to share their experiences and entrust me with critical insights into their challenges and struggles in the building of democratic processes and coalitions across differences.

When I stepped off the bus in Genoa to attend my first meeting leading up to the planned European Social Forum in the summer of 2003, almost all of the houses I saw showed the rainbow-colored *PACE* (peace) flag. Millions of people had been in the streets protesting for global justice and an end to the wars in Afghanistan and Iraq. As I write these lines, many of those whom I met at the time are in the streets again, forming new and even broader coalitions. May this book be a resource for those who give so much of themselves to the work for global justice and real democracy. May they experience the insights and the benefits of political translation both within and beyond their own organizations and groups.

My writing has been informed by fruitful debates with many academic colleagues who lent me their powerful spirit and support. I owe the deepest intellectual debt to three of my teachers who influenced my thinking and my research: Donatella della Porta, who gave me the open ground, the rigor, and the methods that supported my growth; Francesca Polletta, who gave me the conceptual language I needed in order to speak and who read numerous drafts of this work; and Jane Mansbridge, who gave me wings that enabled me to fly by helping me to finalize this book.

Archon Fung, James M. Jasper, Michèle Lamont, and Jackie Smith helped me turn my project into a book and gave me precious feedback on several of the chapters. Marco Oberti, Yves Sintomer, Thomas Risse, and Klaus Eder helped translate the story of this book into a language that speaks to both sociologists and political scientists. I thank Lesley Wood for her stimulating encouragement at different stages of the writing process, and for her in-depth reading and fine theoretical reflections on the finalized manuscript. I thank Nicole Deitelhoff for her support, both as a mentor and as a critical analyst helping me situate this work within international theories of politics and deliberation. I'm grateful to Cathleen Kantner and Patrizia Nanz, whose theories of linguistic and cultural diversity, European politics, and translation were foundational to my research.

I thank Sidney Tarrow for his spirited encouragement at all stages of this research. My warm thanks go to Jeff Juris for his advice and his support throughout, and for his close and critical reading of the finalized manuscript. I thank Jeffrey Alexander, Sean Chabot, Nina Eliasoph, Myra Marx Ferree, Brigitte Geisel, Edwin Gentzler, Jürgen Gerhards, Moira Inghilleri, Mareike Kleine, Amelie Kutter, Sabine Lang, Caroline Lee, Paul Lichterman, Alice Mattoni, Quinton Mayne, Doug McAdam, Deborah Minkoff, Michael McQuarrie, David S. Meyer, Geoffrey Pleyers, Belinda Robnett, Vivien Schmidt, Philip Smith, and Kathrin Zippel for their feedback and support.

I had the great fortune to be supported by my colleagues in the Pioneer Valley and the Five Colleges Social Movement Research Workshop, who commented on numerous earlier versions of this research: Nancy Whittier, Steve Boutcher, Mary Ann Clawson, Rick Fantasia, Jasmine Kerrissey, Joya Misra, Velma Garcia, Daisy Reyes, Marc Steinberg, Carolyn Shread, Kristen Shorette, and Stellan Vintagen. I also had the opportunity to present this work to Bill Gamson, Charlotte Ryan, and the members of the MRAP Research Group in Boston and to the Politics and Protest Workshop in New York City, as well as to the Social Movements Working Group at UC Irvine.

During the final months of writing, I have been generously supported by my colleagues at the University of Copenhagen; I am particularly indebted to the members of the research group on Knowledge, Organization, and Politics, and to Janus Hansen, Michael Hechter, Anders Blok, Mikael Carleheden, Bente Halkier, Peter Gundelach, Jonas Toubøl, and Hans-Jörg Trenz. The members of the Institute for Social Movements and Protest at the Technical University of Berlin have accompanied me since I sat on the bus to Genoa in 2003, and I want to thank in particular Simon Teune, Helena Flam, Dieter Rucht, Anna Cecilia Schwenck, and Elias Steinhilper. I am thankful to Ruth Wodak for her early guidance regarding the critical potential of my research, and to Thorsten Thiel for crucial insights that helped me refine my conceptualization of positional misunderstandings.

Funding by the German Academic Exchange Service provided me with the opportunity to carry out the research described in Chapter 1. A grant by the European Union's Marie Curie Postdoctoral Fellowship Program enabled me to conduct the research for the remaining chapters. I thank the UC Irvine Sociology Department and the UC Irvine Center for the Study of Democracy, who hosted me generously during the fellowship. My research also benefited from a Democracy Fellowship at the Harvard Ash Center for Democratic Governance and Innovation. The central concepts in this book emerged in the context of a vibrant exchange with Archon Fung and the postdocs and doctoral students at the Ash Center and at the Harvard Kennedy School. I am indebted to Sabine Hark and the members of the Center for Research on Women and Gender at the Technical University of Berlin who kindly hosted me during the final phase of manuscript revisions; this support was made possible by research funding provided by the European Union's IPODI grant.

Some material in Chapter 1 appeared previously within "Is 'Another' Public Space Actually Possible? Deliberative Democracy and the Case of 'Women Without,'" *Journal of International Women's Studies* 8(3): 71–87, © 2007; in "Deliberative Discussion, Language, and Efficiency in the World Social Forum Process," *Mobilization* 13(4): 395–410, © 2008; in "Language and Democracy 'in Movement': Multilingualism and the Case of the European Social Forum Process," *Social Movement Studies* 8(2): 149–165, © 2009; in "The Disciplining of Dissent and the Role of Empathetic Listeners in Deliberative Politics: A Ritual Perspective," *Globalizations* 8(4): 519–534, © 2011; and in "Translating Democracy: How Activists in the European Social Forum Practice Multilingual Deliberation," *European Political Science Review* 4(3): 361–384, © 2012. I thank the journal editors and the publishers for permission to reuse the material.

My very special thanks go to Sarah Rabkin for her fine insights and her stimulating critical suggestions as an editor. It has been a joyful journey, and I feel fortunate to have worked with such a terrific editor; she helped me find my voice as an author. I am thankful to the Cambridge University Press editor Robert Dreesen and the Cambridge team and to two anonymous readers for the Press who graciously and generously provided substantive and stylistic comments, and whose close critical reading helped me tremendously.

I thank my friends and my community for holding me – Riqi Kosovske, David Seidenberg, Sally Fuller, Jennifer Levi and her wife Sue, Stacey Novack, Diane O'Donoghue and her wife Kimbell; Mimi, Megan, Beth, Kurt, Leon, Tahera, Millay, Sabine, Isabell, Nadina, Carmen, Uta, Anika, Gesine, Monika and Stefan, Martha, Wilma, and Rainer; and my friends in Eifa: Tanja, Diana, Mario, Carina, Sascha, and Wolfi.

I thank my wife, Noa, for accompanying me with her strong and soft heartbeat as we walk together through this adventurous life, across oceans and over mountains. During the most turbulent times, I could find a refuge in the lands I come from and with my sister Sina and my mom, Elke Fabel Dörr, and her partner Hardy; Noa's parents, David and Hagar; Wölkchen and Clementine; my grandma Rolandi; granddad Willi; Chrissi, Goti, Eva, and Werner; and Noa's aunts and their families.

INTRODUCTION

Addressing Differences and Inequality within Deliberation

Concern for deliberative democracy is sweeping the social sciences, yet real deliberations tend to be far from ideal. Participants and observers who care about the social inequalities that plague many deliberative situations often advocate bringing in third parties to facilitate. But it matters *which* third parties intervene. I analyze the "best case" of a practice that evolved in several radical democracies and one mainstream local democracy to argue that third parties who both understand and advocate for the disadvantaged can frequently be deployed with significant positive effects.

Consider the following scenario, which I observed at a citizen assembly in a Californian city with a population of approximately three hundred thousand I will call Santa Brigida:[1]

"I promise that everyone will be heard tonight," said the facilitator opening the assembly, which took place at city hall.[2] Progressive city council members in Santa Brigida had organized this participatory meeting, as well as earlier citizen forums, to include residents' voices in decision-making on local urban policy. However, just two hours after the facilitator opened the meeting, this promise had already been broken. When it became apparent that city council members, including the facilitator, lacked genuine interest in soliciting citizens' concerns, participating residents expressed their anger publicly. One, Maria Silva,[3] told the facilitator how she saw the problem:

I, Maria, don't feel listened to by you. I have children at home, and I couldn't make dinner for them tonight; they are hungry. If you really wanted to listen, you could sit down at a round table and talk to us. I am so angry. You don't listen to us.

While Maria's speech (delivered in Spanish) reflected what many residents in the assembly felt, the response of the facilitator, who is bilingual but answered in

---

[1] All names in this Introduction are changed.
[2] My fieldnotes, Santa Brigida City Hall meeting, June 7, 2010.   [3] All names changed.

English, seemed to disregard her concerns: "Maria, I ask you to calm down. General comments are not allowed until the end of this session. You must make concrete demands, otherwise we cannot include your concerns." Council members nodded in agreement.

This scene took place in California, but it could easily have occurred in any number of cities throughout the United States or Europe, where policymakers in the past two decades have attempted to promote citizen "empowerment" through public participation and deliberative democracy. In an attempt at reforming mainstream models of representative democracy (where decisions are made by voting), local participatory citizen forums like the one in Santa Brigida are designed to include the proposals of community residents in the decision-making process and are often based on a dialogical or consensus-oriented process of deliberation (Habermas 1984; Mansbridge 1983; Kitschelt 1993; Polletta 2002; Fung 2004; Baiocchi 2005; della Porta 2005; Talpin 2006; Blee 2012; Wood 2012; Lang 2013; Lee 2015; Sintomer et al. 2016). Too often, however, as the case of Maria shows, those for whom these democratic forums are created end up feeling marginalized and misunderstood. *Marginalization*, in this context, occurs within a formally inclusive deliberative process when arguments made by less privileged participants fail to affect outcomes (Young 2003).

Marginalization can result from formal and informal power disparities among participants within ostensibly inclusive and empowering deliberative proceedings. At the Santa Brigida participatory city hall meetings, social-class differences and linguistic barriers divided elected representatives from participating community members – especially poor people; Spanish-speaking immigrants; and women of color, who, like Maria, felt neither heard nor understood by the official facilitator.[4]

When I began this research, I, like many researchers before me, predicted that those who protested about feeling marginalized within the democratic process would choose to leave the meetings where they felt excluded. But this was not the case in Santa Brigida. Following Maria's speech about her frustration with the facilitator, two women in their early twenties distributed leaflets at the back of the assembly. They were local community organizers volunteering as linguistic interpreters/translators for Maria and other immigrant residents who were not native speakers of English, in order to help them understand and participate in the ongoing policy debates taking place at city hall. One of these translators addressed a group of residents who were about to leave the meeting: "We have witnessed how unfair the deliberative process was tonight.

---

[4] I use the broad term *immigrants* to refer to different categories of legal and illegalized (im) migrants in the United States. The broad movement for immigrants' rights in the United States includes different categories of resident immigrants, undocumented immigrants, refugees, and the families and advocates of these groups, including many (undocumented and documented) second-generation immigrants (Chavez 2008).

Together with all local community associations and churches, we have organized an alternative people's forum, the Santa Brigida Community Forum. Several city council members have already agreed to participate. Please join us."[5]

This was not the first intervention by volunteer translators at a Santa Brigida City Hall meeting. While most of the city council members, including the facilitator at the official town hall meeting, were in theory committed to an egalitarian and inclusive process, the community organizers became increasingly aware of how both subtle and more blatant dynamics at those meetings marginalized the voices of many of those for whom they were translating. Working frequently with politicians, those who acted as volunteer translators became aware of their own invisible power positions in these forums. They also discovered the unique power of translators to disrupt the deliberative process without being perceived as out of order, as their official job was to witness and address linguistic miscommunications.

As witnesses and in reaction to the failure of the city hall meetings, community organizers who had worked there as voluntary translators mobilized outraged citizens, other residents, and church groups to establish a community forum that would be chaired and facilitated by the residents. At city hall, city council members had dominated discussion periods with lengthy statements, making it hard for residents to influence decision-making. At the newly created community forum, one of the translators politely interrupted a politician to prevent such dynamics from being repeated: "Excuse me, but you have not answered several questions asked by people here tonight," she stated in English.[6] Another translator then provided a Spanish translation and requested that politicians make concrete concessions to community members. The translators' collective intervention echoed the voices of residents holding protest banners. At this alternative community forum, politicians changed their previously agreed-upon policy proposals following the residents' and translators' collective interventions.

My analysis explains how and why Santa Brigida community translators acted as they did, and how linguistic diversity prompted both their insights and the changes they made in the deliberative process. I analyze *political translation*, distinct from linguistic translation, as a disruptive and communicative practice developed by activists and grassroots community organizers to address the inequities that hinder democratic deliberation, and to entreat powerful groups to work more inclusively with disempowered ones. The insights I derive from the conscious efforts and effects of those who took on the explicit role of political translators in these local forums apply to other situations in which inequalities in communication threaten to undo a democracy.

---

[5] My fieldnotes.　　[6] My fieldnotes.

THE NEGLECTED POWER OF THE THIRD:
POLITICAL TRANSLATORS

Theorists have conceptualized deliberative or communicative democracy as based on direct, egalitarian dialogue that seeks to avoid asymmetrical power. In doing so, they have neglected the powerful informal third position of supposedly neutral facilitators – an omission that has kept us from imagining alternative democratic models. The notion of political translation provides a model for democracy that breaks with the reigning theory of neutral facilitation by adding a specific advocacy role, which I call a *disruptive third position* within political deliberation, in order to foster a more equal and inclusive decision-making process.

At the core of political translation is the translator's unique position as a disruptive third actor between facilitators and conflicting parties. As seen in Maria's case, translators do not seek to act as impartial facilitators; nor are their interventions neutral. Through their witnessing of differences and disagreements between local residents and political elites, including facilitators, the translators in the Santa Brigida case gained a fairly limited yet significant influence over the outcome of the proceedings. They also had the capacity to influence through persuasion, because they understood both the values of the privileged groups and the needs of marginalized ones. Translators used their unique position as a *disruptive third* to influence through persuasion, by directing attention to power imbalances and drawing on the egalitarian commitments of those who otherwise would be unlikely to recognize their own structural privilege.

For residents and community organizers in Santa Brigida, translation has become a model for grassroots democracy and political activism that changes the way in which local deliberation is organized and facilitated. Based on community organizers' and activists' practices as presented in the following chapters, I posit political translation as a twofold model of radical democracy that transcends our conventional understanding of linguistic interpretation in the context of deliberative and participatory citizen forums. First, *political* translators, such as the community organizers in Santa Brigida, come together as a group to resist domination in the context of officially inclusive deliberative or participatory democracy. Rather than boycotting meetings, they openly intervene to challenge cultural and linguistic power asymmetries, within both official community meetings like the one in Santa Brigida and radical democratic meetings created by protesters and social movement groups. Second, political translators also directly intervene within discourse or negotiation to challenge the marginalization that dominant politicians often impose upon disadvantaged community members.

My analysis counters the conventional notion of a "neutral" facilitator role in three ways: first, it shows that in the context of all of the cases I studied, deliberative groups with only "neutral" facilitators tended to fail. Second, it shows that the political translators succeeded by acquiring both an oppositional consciousness and effective political power through their positions as witnessing, disruptive third parties and their ability to act at least somewhat independently of dominant interests. Third, it documents three conditions that make political translation effective: a context of cultural and linguistic differences; a commitment to equality among some privileged group members; and, most importantly, the translators' development of a disruptive third position.

POLITICAL TRANSLATION AND SOCIAL MOVEMENTS

Translators' political role has been described by theorists of comparative literature, culture, feminism, language, and Marxist philosophy (Venuti 1992; Sakai 1997; Tymocko 1999; Gentzler and Tymocko 2002; Gentzler 2008; Apter 2006; Boéri 2010; Baker 2016; Butler 1999; Conway 2011; Nanz 2006; Santos 2005; Mezzadra 2007). Translators' critical interventions in public discourse vary depending on the specific context of interaction (Gentzler 2007). In historical revolutionary moments and postcolonial contexts, literary translators have taken on an important role by translating and spreading new terms and subversive political meanings to popular audiences (Tymoczko 1999, 2007; Baker 2016). With the rise of popular influence on power holders through digital and social media, activists in the Egyptian revolution have used linguistic translation and subtitling as a way to broadcast independent news and alternative meanings to transnational audiences of supporters (Baker 2016).

Belying an abstract, normative conception of a neutral, impartial translation, empirical research reveals a degree of agency as well as situated moral judgments on the part of interpreters operating in power-dominated arenas for public dialogue. For example, in asylum interviews or in court hearings involving detained undocumented immigrants, translators may find themselves in the ethically challenging position of being the only individuals to fully grasp the failures of mutual dialogue that arise from prejudices involving categories such as gender, race, or class, among others (Inghilleri 2012; Mokre 2015). While professional interpreters' training prepares them to act as impartial mediators to ensure that speakers and hearers understand each other, impartiality and neutrality may in reality limit translators' capacity to transmit the truth across linguistic and cultural boundaries (Inghilleri 2012).

An increasing number of professional linguistic translators and volunteer interpreters currently use their language skills to engage in social protest, engendering a need for research on how translators can influence political processes of discourse, deliberation, and democratic decision-making. This is a rich and generative field, within which I have pursued one rather particular line of inquiry. Following translation theorist Moira Inghilleri, I use the notions of translating and interpreting interchangeably in this book to emphasize the cultural component of the work of both interpreters and translators (Inghilleri 2012). Rather than focus on the political ramifications of linguistic translation or interpreting per se, I look at *political translation* as a broad set of practices designed to address marginalization based on gender, class, race, and other differences – even within groups whose members speak the same language. For example, I will show that US global justice activists used the concept of translation to describe their radical democratic contributions to building a broader US American Left coalition connecting climate justice activists and NGOs close to the Democratic Party with undocumented immigrants, excluded workers, LGBT leaders of color, and minority organizers.

Political translation presents a new way to theorize the political role of activists who engage in deliberative politics. Activists bring to deliberative forums a critical awareness that counterbalances the subtle and overt influences that economic and political interests exert on public decision makers (Polletta 2015). From an activist perspective, though, deliberative forums actually risk co-opting and delegitimizing protest: for example, if a facilitator marginalizes the perspective of already disenfranchised groups (Young 2003). Moreover, the presence of political activists within citizen forums is contested (Polletta 2015). As Francesca Polletta shows, some deliberative democrats argue that protest is necessary if deliberation fails to be inclusive, if it is biased or unfair, and if it does little but reproduce elite discourse (Smith 2004; Habermas 1981). Others, however, fear that protesters could impede the deliberative process if they only advocate for their own political ideas – failing to engage in serious dialogue with other groups (Talisse 2001; see, for a discussion, Polletta 2015).

Addressing some of these open questions, political translation provides a perspective for activists to engage within deliberative politics without being perceived as threatening to the norms of deliberation and yet in a way that challenges inequity within public discourse. Activists who intervene as political translators do more than protesters speaking for social justice. By translating on behalf of other groups or individuals, activists transcend their own group's particular position. They acquire a new role within deliberative forums through their position as a third party challenging cultural and social hierarchies in deliberative and participatory democratic settings.

Political translation draws on two different conceptions of power in communication: the liberal assumption that deliberation will inevitably lead to fair and equitable decisions through mutual persuasion, and the radical perspective that posits a need to disrupt existing power structures in order to make such outcomes possible. Behind these contrasting conceptions of power lie two different notions of equality: unlike the liberal point of view, the radical position assumes that playing fields require leveling before all factions can participate equally. Political translators act from a liberal perspective when they echo and support arguments made by marginalized group members; they take a more radical approach when they collectively disrupt and interrupt deliberations in which dominant groups marginalize disadvantaged group members.

As political translators, activists challenge the ideals of neutrality and impartiality in situations that many participants in a meeting perceive as unfair, in which a dominant group systematically ignores demands for equality and justice made by another, less privileged group. I call such situations *positional misunderstandings*. At their core lie material differences of interest entangled with inequality.

The *positional* misunderstanding between Maria and the facilitator at Santa Brigida's local democratic forum reflects a larger debate about inequality and democratic participation that divides institutional leaders and engaged citizens. In radical democratic theory, Jacques Rancière has used the notion of "disagreement" to describe the failure of consensus-based and deliberative democratic models to effectively include demands for greater equality and social justice made by the less privileged (Rancière 1995). While deliberative democracy has become the mainstream model for policy-makers and progressive institutions aiming to enhance citizen dialogue, the democratic outcomes of deliberative reforms have been contested (Fraser 2007; Lee et al. 2015). Those who have studied the diffusion of deliberative models from small local citizen forums to broader national political arenas are concerned about the instrumentalization and increasing commercialization of such practices (Lee et al. 2015). Today, deliberation is a key model for negotiation used by mainstream political institutions, such as the European Union, as well as by development companies, multinational corporations, and international financial institutions, such as the International Monetary Fund, which adopt deliberative models as a way of enhancing transparency and accountability (see, critically, Fraser 2007; Eliasoph 2011, 2015; Deitelhoff 2012; Deitelhoff and Thiel 2014; Lang 2013; Lee 2015). Critical research suggests that the mainstreaming of deliberative democracy may not facilitate "empowerment"; rather, it may serve as a tool for power holders to legitimate themselves (Nanz and Steffek 2004; Deitelhoff 2012; Lang 2013, 2015; Lee et al. 2015; McQuarrie 2015).

My critique in this book is different. I do not address the intentional manipulation of deliberative democratic forms of participation by dominant interests. Rather, I look at places where deliberation goes wrong even when people genuinely attempt to make it work. To understand the puzzle that positional misunderstandings create, I analyze mainstream deliberative settings created by policy-makers as well as alternative forums for radical democracy and consensus-based decision-making created by protesters, community organizers, or local residents, such as Maria. In many of these groups, facilitators were supposedly motivated to include everyone in the process and were clearly sympathetic to the concerns of those included in the democratic deliberation process. Nevertheless, these facilitators marginalized, often preconsciously, the people they sought to include.

In Santa Brigida the problem was even greater than the facilitator's failure to help participants. In fact, the misunderstanding between the facilitator and residents in Santa Brigida involved linguistic and cultural barriers that prevented the emergence of an inclusive democratic debate between residents and city council members. Democratic theories have assumed that a shared language is a necessary background condition for democratic discourse. Yet in Santa Brigida, only the official facilitator and city council members spoke English, while the majority of residents present had to rely on volunteer translators.

Santa Brigida's efforts at democratic deliberation point to a broader concern about political communication. How can people work together across cultural differences in increasingly multilingual, multicultural societies? Regarding the case of Europe and of multilingual nation-states, cosmopolitan and deliberative theorists have advanced English as a shared language, a "lingua franca" for transnational democratic communication (Habermas 1996; Archibugi 2005; Dryzek 2009; Van Parijs 2011). However, from a multicultural and communitarian perspective, civic deliberation, in order to be truly democratic and inclusive, needs to take place in people's authentic language, their local vernacular (Kymlicka 2001); otherwise public discourse reifies cultural misrecognition and linguistic colonialism (Taylor 1995).

I suggest, as an intervention in this ongoing debate, that whether a single global language or multiple local languages are involved in deliberations, the need to uncover inequality and bridge difference remains. People have unquestioned, familiar ways of understanding or misunderstanding each other that can determine how culture enables and restricts cooperation in heterogeneous groups (Polletta 2002, 2008). With political translation, I present a practice that produced dramatic results in improving the inclusivity and effectiveness of decision-making practices in diverse movement groups and local democratic settings. Political translation can turn real differences among deliberating groups into a resource for deepening democracy.

THE POTENTIAL OF MULTILINGUAL, CULTURALLY DIVERSE DEMOCRACY IN SOCIAL MOVEMENTS

I began my analysis of political translation by trying to understand how those groups that objected to marginalization within official deliberative forums would work within their own culturally diverse groups and grassroots democratic assemblies (della Porta 2005a, 2009, 2012; della Porta and Rucht 2009; Polletta 2002; Blee 2012; Smith 2007; Wood 2012). Activists engaged in the global justice movement in Europe and the United States have used political translation to address positional misunderstandings in the context of radical democratic, consensus-oriented, deliberative democracy, set in multilingual meetings and transnational assemblies that involve people with a multiplicity of identities and linguistic backgrounds (della Porta 2005b; Doerr 2008, 2012; Klein 2008). One particularly important model of egalitarian, grassroots-based democracy and deliberation is the World Social Forum (WSF). Created in 2001 by activists working on global justice, the WSF is the largest transnational face-to-face experiment in radical democracy at the time of this study (della Porta 2012; Juris 2008a, 2008b; Pleyers 2010; Smith et al. 2007, 2012; Smith 2007; Smith and Wiest 2012; Teivainen 2002; Whitaker 2004). For eight years I studied decision-making and deliberation in the WSF's regional Social Forums in Europe and the United States, which involved thousands of citizens, immigrants, and multilingual speakers discussing social justice and global politics.

I assumed that deliberation in monolingual, national social and citizen forums in Europe and the United States would be more inclusive and more democratically successful than in groups facing linguistic disparities. Most studies of deliberative democracy would make such a prediction, assuming that a multiplicity of languages would obstruct the deliberative process. Drawing on eight years of ethnographic fieldwork (2003–2010) involving case studies of forty Social Forum meetings and local citizen forums in the United States, Germany, Italy, France, and the United Kingdom, however, I discovered that – as this book will show – linguistically and culturally diverse groups were actually *more* inclusive in their democratic processes and decision-making outcomes than homogeneous groups, and they also survived longer. The explanation for this counterintuitive finding lies in the process of political translation.

Even though linguistic difference is often seen as a hindrance to democratic deliberation, in the cases I studied, this difference was designated by all participating parties as an issue that needed to be addressed, and thus prompted efforts to discuss the potential problems it might cause. In attempting to address linguistic problems, the participants opened up an avenue for better understanding the *positional* misunderstandings that so often distort deliberation between members of privileged and disadvantaged groups. In all of the monolingual groups that I studied, positional misunderstandings led to internal crises and to the groups' decisions to break into different factions. As a result of the explicit attention that both multilingual and highly diverse deliberative settings drew to cultural differences among participants, these settings also inspired political translation, the collective practice of openly challenging and tackling positional misunderstandings within deliberative politics.

The political translation practices that this study uncovers have not been previously addressed by democratic theorists, and they bring to the foreground people's grassroots engagement with positional misunderstandings and structural inequality in the context of cultural and linguistic diversity. Political translation builds on previous experiences and radical democratic practices of social movements that for both ethical and strategic purposes saw the process of deliberation as being at least as important as the outcome (della Porta 2005a). In different generations of protest, students in the civil rights movement, feminists, anarchists, and global justice activists have addressed the issue of power within consensus practices requiring norms for facilitators to pay attention to the way that structural inequalities play out within a meeting (Phillips 1993; Whittier 1995; Polletta 2002; Young 1996, 2000, 2003). Radical democrats and anarchists who formed part of the global justice movement and who founded the North American Direct Action Network worked with *third facilitators* to ensure their network included and prioritized the voices of marginalized participants (Polletta 2002). Deliberative theorists and social movement scholars have only started to explore immigrants' and activists' grassroots attempts to address the reality of multilingual policy-making in the context of local urban democracy and transnational political participation (Nanz 2006, 2009; Alcalde 2015). Sociologists draw attention to the key role of social movement activists as translators who spread ideas from one national political context to another (Chabot 2012; Levitt and Merry 2007). My study will not specifically focus on translation as the diffusion or adaptation of ideas across different contexts (Chabot 2012). I also use "translation" differently than does Boaventura de Sousa Santos, who conceives of it as a counterhegemonic normative ideal (Santos 2006; see, for a discussion, Conway 2011). Rather, I will restrict my focus to the political practice of translation as used by community organizers in Santa Brigida and activists in social movements for their radical democratic practices. In comparing deliberation in meetings with or without political translation, I will begin to identify conditions under which heterogeneous groups may work together more democratically.

POLITICAL TRANSLATION VERSUS NEUTRAL FACILITATION

I will make several arguments regarding both positional misunderstandings and political translation within deliberation, based on one case of local mainstream democracy in California and on several radical democracies set in the WSF process and its American and European chapters. First, I will show that egalitarian democracy and deliberation often fail to fulfill their tasks because they do not address the problem of marginalization within the model of consensus-based democracy. Second, focusing on practices of political translation, I will show how social justice activists and community organizers in both the United States and Europe have worked to institutionalize a *disruptive third voice* within deliberation that helps members of marginalized groups influence and alter processes of facilitation and decision-making perceived as being "unfair." Third, I will show how the grassroots practice of political translation provides a better model for equal deliberation than is found in any model of neutral facilitation in the cases I discuss. I will argue that political translation helps to solve positional misunderstandings regarding race, gender, class, and language differences or other cultural differences. These misunderstandings remain unseen within models of neutral facilitation and, in turn, impede democratic deliberation.

POLITICAL TRANSLATION: WHAT THIS BOOK WILL COVER

To examine how positional misunderstandings occur, I analyze case studies in which activists and community organizers employed political translation to counter the marginalization of disadvantaged groups in participatory-styled proceedings and deliberative forums. In Chapter 1, I trace the conditions that led to the emergence, and subsequent influence, of a political translation collective in the multilingual, transnational arena of the European Social Forum (ESF). The ESF, as part of the broader WSF, provides a good case for studying facilitation and positional misunderstandings involving citizens and immigrants from across Europe and the European Union. ESF grassroots activists who were acting as volunteer linguistic translators witnessed and sought to address inequality caused by positional misunderstandings in multilingual European assemblies. I compare deliberations that took place in multinational, multilingual ESF preparatory assembly meetings with those at the (monolingual) national preparatory meetings in Italy, Germany, and the United Kingdom.

I argue that the relative inclusiveness of multinational, multilingual group processes arises from the oppositional consciousness, leverage, and communicative power created by a political translation collective that emerged as a result of the linguistic and cultural differences at the multinational ESF level. Building on their official role as the "Babels interpreters and translators" in the European meetings, volunteer translators collectively and publicly resisted unfair decisions and temporarily interrupted their linguistic service to represent the voices of marginalized participants. This collective drew on volunteer translators' experiential knowledge of positional misunderstandings that are often preconscious in nature and occur based on subtle or more obvious power imbalances among the involved parties. Political translation drew on the Babels' collective force as a heterogeneous multilingual and pluralist network, working to intervene as a disruptive third voice within the deliberation.[7]

Considering that linguistic diversity and overlapping cultural misunderstandings factored prominently in the political translation collective at the ESF meetings, Chapter 2 assesses ways in which political translation could also be applicable in more homogeneous, traditionally monolingual political-debate environments. I begin with an analysis of the United States Social Forum (USSF), which is, at the time of this study, one of the most culturally diverse face-to-face forums for civic deliberation on global justice and inequality within the United States, involving nearly twenty thousand participants as of 2010. USSF organizers were global justice activists, many of them people of color, who had attended the WSF and recognized that they could use political translation as a tool to prevent marginalization based on race and other distinctions in settings that do not necessarily require linguistic translation.

In 2003 misunderstandings related to issues of race undermined the first attempt to organize a Social Forum in the United States, fomenting a political crisis that ended cooperation among local grassroots global justice groups that mobilized immigrants, minorities, and poor people; professional national

---

[7] My fieldnotes.

NGOs; and movement organizations. However, as occurred at multinational ESF meetings, this crisis inspired the development of a critical political translation collective. In an exceptional move, (minority) linguistic translators and cultural intermediaries, who had tried to reconnect the divided factions, came together from across the United States to accomplish something that the existing parties had been unable to achieve: the creation of a nationwide social movement coalition, the USSF. With almost a decade of data analysis, my ethnographic comparison shows how these political translators' interruptions and critical interventions during USSF national preparatory meetings helped resolve internal crises over finances, ideology, and identity – discussions of a kind that dramatically failed in the various Social Forum cases I studied in Europe. Chapter 2, in short, shows how political translation helped movement coalitions both to survive internal communication breakdowns and collapse and to broaden their outreach to new members and organizations.

After comparing political translation collectives in transnational, multilingual settings and national monolingual settings in European and American contexts, I leave the arena of movement politics to explore whether political translation could also be an effective tool for deliberative politics in institutional settings at the local level. In Chapter 3, I return to the dilemma that prevented the effective inclusion of immigrant residents in community deliberations, such as with the case with Maria in Santa Brigida. In two similar yet contrasting examples of progressive American politics in this Californian city, I analyze the effectiveness of political translation involving either institutional insiders or independent civic translators. In the first case, a number of progressive city council members in Santa Brigida wanted to empower residents by hosting a deliberative process at city hall on an urban planning project. Because they were bilingual in both English and Spanish (the native language of many residents), city council members saw themselves as institutional political translators and acted, in essence, as facilitators promising to listen to local interested parties. Because many of those present at the meeting spoke only either English or Spanish, the council members paid for bilingual interpretation and also allowed community members to bring their own translators. Yet despite these provisions, decisionmakers and bilingual facilitators ignored almost all of the questions about the project raised by residents, not to mention any alternative proposals. At the end of deliberation, residents expressed frustration about being ignored, and left. This case shows how self-proclaimed institutional political translators failed when, after assuming positions of power, they started to systematically ignore residents' demands.

The second comparative case, presented in Chapter 4, involved the same actors as in Chapter 3, but in this case the meetings were moved to an alternate setting: The Santa Brigida Community Forum, where the roles of representatives and political translators were distinguished as separate entities and local residents were empowered as a result of the interventions of political translators. The forum was to be chaired and facilitated by the immigrant residents who were directly affected by the planning project under discussion, which had caused resident evictions. Residents themselves visibly took responsibility for all of the central roles as facilitators, chairs, and civic experts. Doing little more than changing informal role hierarchies and enabling critical interventions through the role of the *disruptive third*, this conscious political translation method dramatically changed the tenor of the deliberations, since no facilitator or official was able to interrupt residents' speeches. While one would expect local democracy to be most inclusive if disadvantaged local residents have elected their own representatives, this comparison reveals the persistent need for grassroots political translators who are able to build a third, communicative space for radical democracy that interrupts the dualist power structure and asymmetric roles between decision-makers and the less privileged.

In the Conclusion, I unite my findings based on the three case-study examinations. The theory of political translation that I advance here provides an empirical account of the conditions that foster the emergence of political translation collectives and their empowering potential for democracy. My central argument is that truly democratic deliberation involving diverse groups depends on the institutionalization of a third position for political translation. The collectives of political translators that I saw emerge independently in both Europe and the United States sought not only to disrupt and challenge cultural and social hierarchies within existing deliberative models of neutral facilitation and cultural mediation but also to use political translation as a foundational model for democracy – a democracy that stems from the need to reconcile inequality and misunderstandings based on differences.

In summary, my findings show that the structural conditions necessary for effective political translation are (a) an existing stalemate or political deliberation crisis and neutral facilitation, (b) a shared perception by political translators of positional misunderstandings as the origin of the crisis, and (c) political translators' willingness to collectively intervene. What defines linguistic and/or cultural translators as *political translators* is their ability to enact collective, conscious, disruptive interventions that challenge dominant social relations – a practice that contradicts the commitment to neutrality in facilitation and deliberation.

Political translators do not necessarily have to be linguistic interpreters. They can also work on translating race, gender, or class differences. Chapter 2 shows how a grassroots political translation collective that emerged in the context of the USSF challenged positional misunderstandings arising from differences of race, class, and gender in national coalition meetings involving professionalized NGOs and local, grassroots-based minority groups. In Chapter 4, political translators also challenge positional misunderstandings based on class differences. Notably, in all cases studied, political translation united isolated and marginalized participants from a variety of cultural groups into a powerful "third-voice" group: political translators who by dint of their witnessing positions could testify to hidden inequalities.

Still, as shown in Chapter 3, political translation will fail if some of its protagonists, even those who have experienced marginalization, assume leadership positions and claim to "speak for" disadvantaged participants despite having dominant positions in institutional power structures. The limitations of political translation are practical as well as strategic: its interventions complicate and lengthen meetings, and political translation may be difficult to implement in homogeneous groups (Chapter 2). Taking these challenges into consideration, I assess political translation's power to reconnect the arenas of social justice, deliberative democracy, and discursive practices at the intersections of participation, protest, and policy-making in increasingly multilingual, globalized societies.

I

Paris

A Political Translation Collective Emerges

Social movements in Europe protesting the EU's austerity policies are growing apace – but current movements have trouble crossing national boundaries while right-wing and nationalist mobilizations are on the rise (della Porta 2012; Wodak 2015). Many observers see linguistic barriers as the primary impediment to alliance-building among groups in different countries that share the same grievances (Rucht 2002; Tarrow 2006). This chapter shows that *political translation* as a democratic practice can help social movement groups transcend such barriers by actually building on linguistic differences in order to work successfully together.

Imagine Paris in summer of 2003: In the wake of widespread street protests throughout Europe, hundreds of global justice activists from Rome, Berlin, Madrid, London, Warsaw, and other cities have descended on the French capital to debate a radical democratic European Constitution envisioning social and civic rights for both citizens and immigrants. The context is the "European Social Forum," a transnational civic assembly designed to be "open to all." Tonight, however, some participants are asking, "Why do the French and German groups get twice as many seats in the plenary assembly as Eastern Europeans?" "Why do women and migrants get so few seats?"[1] The facilitator, a member of one of the most influential groups represented at the forum, fails to respond substantively to these questions. A stalemate develops. Into this troubled scene, a group of volunteer linguistic translators, normally invisible at the back of the assembly, intervene. "This 'consensus' proposal is not fair," they say. "We translators have decided not to continue translating until the rules are changed." The assembly cannot go on. The disruption prompts a hurried discussion among the organizers, after which the facilitator announces that from now on women will get half the seats on all national lists and that the German delegation will share its seats with immigrants and other resource-poor groups.

[1] My fieldnotes, ESF preparatory assembly, Paris Bobigny, September 29, 2003.

This was the first openly critical public intervention on behalf of the translators. Although all of the participants in this forum and earlier European assemblies were committed in theory to an egalitarian and inclusive process, the members who had volunteered to serve as translators had become increasingly aware of how both subtle and unsubtle dynamics at the meetings marginalized the voices of many for whom they were translating. At the same time, they were beginning to perceive their own invisible leverage in these forums. They had discovered that because their official task was to witness and address linguistic miscommuni-cations, translators possessed a unique power to disrupt the process without being perceived as acting out of order. They also had the capacity to influence through persuasion, because they understood both the values of the privileged groups and the needs of the marginalized.

This chapter explains how and why these translators acted as they did, and how the linguistic heterogeneity they addressed prompted both their critical insights and the subsequent capacities of the social movement groups that founded the European Social Forum (ESF) to work together democratically in a transnational, asymmetric, and heterogeneous setting.

Created in 2002, the Forum had mobilized a series of massive protests against the EU's neoliberal political agenda, connecting unions, members of the European Parliament, and grassroots activists (della Porta and Caiani 2009; Doerr 2012, see also Dufour 2010). Its members had then decided to design a radical democratic counterproposal for a European Constitution that would include a Charter for Social Rights (ESF 2008; cf. Dufour 2010). In addition, they made decisions about jointly organized Europe-wide and global action days, positions on specific EU policies and campaigns, and joint protest initiatives in 2003, 2004, and 2005 (Doerr 2012). By attending and analyzing twenty of these meetings, I was able to discover why some succeeded. These insights apply more broadly to democracy and deliberation in many other settings.

My research began with an empirical puzzle. In the eleven Europe-wide Social Forum assemblies I studied, citizens from different countries, speaking different languages and feeling like strangers to each other, seemed able to work together *more* democratically than citizens in the nine monolingual national Social Forum meetings I attended. Most studies of deliberative democracy would predict that many languages would obstruct the work of the Europe-wide assemblies. Like many others, at the beginning of my research I too assumed that deliberation in the multinational, multilingual ESF meetings would be less inclusive and less successful democratically, as a result of linguistic differences, than in the national-level Social Forum meetings. From 2003 to 2010, I studied these meetings, some of which included native speakers of over ten different languages, including German, French, Italian, Spanish, Greek, Portuguese, Hungarian, Polish, Russian, Arabic, and Turkish. I compared deliberations that took place in multinational, multilingual ESF assemblies with those that took place at national meetings in Italy, Germany, and the United Kingdom. I was surprised to discover that, contrary to my expectations, the multilingual international assemblies worked better and had many more democratic elements than the national ones.

My counterintuitive finding derives from a dynamic of conscious attention based on some key participants' successful exploitation of an unexpected source of power. Because both multilingual and highly diverse European assemblies drew explicit attention to cultural differences among participants, these meetings also inspired "political translation," a collective practice in which linguistic translators openly challenged what I call *positional misunderstandings*. Such misunderstandings, based on structural inequities rather than on linguistic communication problems, often characterize interactions between members of privileged and disadvantaged groups within deliberative politics. The misunderstanding at the European assembly in Paris was a positional misunderstanding: at its core was inequality dividing wealthy national and political groups from others. At the heart of this conflict, we shall see, was the reluctance of influential and affluent groups at the European assembly to treat less privileged group members as equals within the deliberative process.

I use the term *political translation*, as distinct from linguistic translation, to denote what I construe to be a disruptive and communicative practice developed by ESF activists, whose acts of translation addressed the inequities that hindered both democratic deliberation and mutual understanding between groups with unequal power. In attempting to redress linguistic problems, the translators created a mode of interaction that allowed all participants to analyze and respond to the characteristic misunderstandings that derive from power differences among participants. In all of the monolingual national Social Forum groups that I studied, positional misunderstandings led to internal democratic crises, with groups separating into different factions. In the multilingual international Social Forums the critical interventions of political translators transformed this internal dynamic.

GRASSROOTS DEMOCRACY, MARGINALIZATION, AND INEQUALITY WITHIN SOCIAL MOVEMENTS

The political translation that took place at the ESF is a radical democratic practice. It emerged as a direct response to deliberative democracy's shortcomings, which arise in the practices of consensus-based decision-making in many social movement groups. In the consensus-based democracy of the ESF, direct, immediate deliberation among speakers is the dominant ideal (della Porta 2005a; Maeckelbergh 2009; Smith 2007; Smith et al. 2007; ESF 2008). The speakers are expected to present arguments that promote mutual understanding despite differences, with consensus being reached through an inclusive, "horizontal," transparent, and egalitarian debate (Smith et al. 2007; della Porta 2005a; Juris 2013; Flesher Fominaya 2015). However, experience has shown that despite the best intentions of those attempting to institute a form of democracy that is direct, grassroots-based, and fair to all, challenges arise from informal, often-hidden power differentials that can lead to inequality in the deliberative process (Freeman 1972; Young 1996, 2003; della Porta 2005a; Blee 2012; Maeckelbergh 2009; Wood 2012; Flesher Fominaya 2015; Polletta 2015). Theorists and activists alike have demonstrated in these settings the informal power of institutional elites, including the members of powerful national delegations who establish themselves as facilitators (Maeckelbergh 2004; Nuñes 2005; Reyes 2006; Wrainwright 2006; Doerr 2007).

My analysis of inequality and informal marginalization begins with the 2003 ESF Paris assembly. I show how the linguistic translators at the Paris assembly intervened collectively as a third actor, facilitating discussion between the official facilitator and participants who felt marginalized. The translators intervened to address not only linguistic but *positional misunderstandings*: discursive processes through which dominant group members, including facilitators, publicly deny disadvantaged groups the relevance of their political arguments for greater equality. In Paris a critical mass of participants perceived the facilitators as protecting the interests of a privileged few. At the assembly in 2003, frustrated linguistic translators initiated an intervention to address the entrenched inequities and informal marginalization within purportedly democratic decision-making processes; that is, they took on the role of political translators. This informal action in 2003 attracted members of many resource-poor activist groups in the ESF and launched a political translation collective.

Collectively, the translators learned to work together to intervene as a disruptive third voice within the ESF deliberations. Unlike the meeting facilitator, the political translators were in a unique position to challenge informal domination. Building on their official role as linguistic translators in the European meetings, the volunteer translators soon collectively and publicly resisted unfair decisions by temporarily interrupting their linguistic services to elevate the voices of marginalized participants and groups.

My comparison of deliberation in the national and the European meetings shows how political translation can provide a model for radical democracy that breaks with the reigning theory of neutral facilitation by adding a specific advocacy role, which I call a *disruptive third position* within political deliberation, in order to foster a more equal and inclusive decision-making process.

What distinguishes my political translation model from other existing theories of what I call *the third* within deliberation is that I do not suggest reconstructing facilitation to better assure its neutrality. Nor do I recommend replacing facilitators with other cultural intermediaries more capable of being neutral. Rather, I show that deliberation is more productive when it includes political translators who are motivated to expose power differentials and other issues that contribute to positional misunderstandings. Political translators are able to facilitate a more equitable process because their experience leads them to become aware of the ways in which "neutral" settings of political deliberation are laced with forms of unequal access and other features of marginalization. In order to further analyze the place of the third within political deliberation, I explore the informal power positions of both the "neutral" moderating facilitators and the linguistic translators who became political translators in the ESF process.

This chapter will describe the European Social Forum – its participants, its mission, and how it functioned within and among the many participating countries – and the group of linguistic translators known as the Babels. I present a case study that examines how and why individuals who considered themselves committed to equality failed at facilitating inclusive and transparent deliberation despite their good intentions, and I trace how this and other conditions led to the emergence and influence of a group of political translators in the transnational arena of the ESF. Through an analysis of translators' perceptions and their changing role in the deliberation process, I discuss the factors that contributed to the success of this political translation intervention, and I consider the potential of power misuse by political translators. Finally, I consider how political translation could be a tool for fostering equity and inclusion in other democratic processes.

THE EUROPEAN SOCIAL FORUM: A GRASSROOTS DEMOCRATIC EXPERIMENT

The ESF was the largest multilingual grassroots democracy experiment "from below" that had ever taken place in Europe. From 2002 to 2010, the ESF brought together thousands of global justice activists and members of unions and leftist parties both within individual countries and in Europe-wide meetings. Its sustained, nearly decade-long period of face-to-face meetings makes the ESF unique in the history of social movements in Europe to date (della Porta 2005a; della Porta and Caiani 2009; della Porta 2009; Rucht 2009; Haug et al. 2009; Pleyers 2010). While other protesters, such as those who opposed anti-austerity measures in Europe, lacked transnational arenas in which to connect face to face despite years of organizing, the ESF succeeded in building a lively multinational, multilingual democratic Social Forum involving thousands of protesters (della Porta 2012). Parallel national Social Forum meetings based within individual countries, however, collapsed.

Created in 2002 as a transnational arena for deliberation about the future of "another Europe," the ESF, over the next eight years, brought together dozens of Europe-wide campaigns organized by activists from many countries. The first ESF summit took place in 2002 in Florence with one million participants, followed by annual or semiannual ESF summits with hundreds of thousands of participants in Paris (2003), London (2004), Athens (2006), Malmö (2008), and Istanbul (2010). In order to develop these summits, the ESF initiated a huge organizational effort in which thousands of global justice activists participated in preparatory meetings within both national chapters and European-wide assemblies. Participation in these meetings was fluid and extremely diverse. For example, three hundred participants attended the European preparatory assembly in Paris, described above, while only one hundred fifty attended a follow-up European preparatory assembly in London, organized in mid-December, 2003.

Comparing European and national preparatory meetings, I noted a similar political spectrum of groups and participants present and similar lines of political conflict. More than half of the activists who typically participated in European and national preparatory meetings belonged to leftist unions and Left-leaning party associations and saw themselves as socialists, social democrats, Marxists, or Trotskyites, a finding that is confirmed in two participant surveys (Andretta and Reiter 2009). The remainder of participants in these meetings – such as ecologists, autonomous activists, anarchists, feminists, and lesbian and gay groups – saw themselves as part of "new" social movements, and/or as part of networks that emerged within the global justice movement (Doerr 2009).

About half of the participants in the European preparatory assemblies came from resource-poor local groups – that is, they were grassroots activists as opposed to paid professional activists. For several reasons these activists viewed participation at the multinational assemblies as sufficiently important to merit overcoming the economic and logistical difficulties involved in attending. First, the issues debated at the national meetings were also being debated at the European assemblies, and central issues were co-decided. Second, the European preparatory assembly was the highest decision-making body of the ESF, and it would routinely override decisions made at the national level of preparatory meetings (Maeckelbergh 2004; Doerr 2009; Haug et al. 2009). Aware of this policy, grassroots activists who were determined to ensure representation of their positions on particular issues mobilized all available resources to travel to the European assembly meetings. Consequently, the same lines of conflict occurring at national meetings were reproduced at the European level (Doerr 2009; Maeckelbergh 2004).

The types of decisions being made at preparatory meetings could be categorized into three areas: logistics, finances, and politics. The European assembly also negotiated consensus agreements when various national factions in each country were divided in their opinions (Doerr 2007; Maeckelbergh 2004; Nuñes 2005). For the period I studied, these issues included ESF finances, venue host cities, meeting agendas, relevant discussion topics, and speaker lists, which would determine who would be invited to present at upcoming ESF summits. For example, the European preparatory assembly held in Paris co-decided with national preparatory meetings the locations of upcoming ESF summits, as well as each national "speaker list" identifying who would be invited to participate at the ESF summit that was to take place in Paris in November 2003. These were controversial decisions passionately debated among participating activists, who were often divided along similar party lines. Indeed, political battles at both European and national meetings typically involved conflict between two main factions: professional activists, who typically worked for unions and political parties, and grassroots activists, who typically came from resource-poor local activist and immigrant groups.

This division was also reflected in the roles participants took on at meetings. While professional activists assumed positions as meeting facilitators, the rank-and-file members of the unions and political parties as well as grassroots activists who worked for local, resource-poor groups did not. Conflicts revolved around finances and political themes in all of the European and national meetings that I attended. Grassroots activists, many of them committed anarchists, feminists, or ecologists, often found themselves in the position of asking institutional leftists to provide better access to information and a more equal distribution of resources. These often-unrecognized power imbalances, combined with overlapping conflicts related to issues of identity and ideology, led to repeated positional misunderstandings.

TRANSLATORS AND THE POSITION OF THE DISRUPTIVE THIRD IN MULTILINGUAL DELIBERATION

I shall analyze the extraordinary communicative power of participants who met together at the European assemblies and united as a collective of political translators intervening to address informal marginalization and power asymmetries within these venues. By exploring how political translators came to act collectively, this analysis broadens our understanding of the power of collective action set in the context of discursive or deliberative settings. Neglected in existing theories about the role of the neutral third in deliberation is how the transformative cultural and political power of translation is relevant to global or transnational deliberative arenas, particularly in its ability to foster transparency and inclusivity.

Because the multinational European assemblies included participants who spoke many different languages, they required linguistic translation. To meet this need, grassroots participants who had also been involved in local and national meetings and who were students of professional interpretation stepped forward to volunteer in this role (Boéri and Hodkinson 2004; Boéri 2010; Doerr 2007, 2009). These volunteer translators ultimately joined forces to form an organization they called Babels. The presence of the Babels translators improved access in particular for participants who only spoke their home language. It was also useful for participants in general, two-thirds of whom reported making use of the real-time interpretation because of their difficulties in comprehending the variety of languages being spoken.[2] This wide

---

[2] My survey conducted in the European preparatory meetings shows that among the participants who answered my questionnaires, nearly two-thirds evaluated themselves as being able to speak English fluently (63 percent), while 10 percent said they did not speak English at all (Doerr 2009).

reliance on simultaneous interpretation had the effect of creating a multivocal space composed of several working languages, including English, French, German, Greek, Italian, Spanish, and, for a notable number of participants, also Turkish.

Initially, the students of simultaneous interpretation volunteered to translate at the European assemblies in order to address inequities that they saw stemming from language barriers. Arnaud,[3] a founding member of the Babels, described the group's inception this way:

> The idea to found Babels came up when, during an international meeting, a woman from Kirgizstan from a human rights organization made a statement. She noticed that nobody could understand her. She became more and more desperate . . . All listened but nobody understood. That is why we as students of simultaneous interpretation created Babels.[4]

Babels volunteers, such as Arnaud, believed that language barriers increased asymmetries of power and access to information between participants at the European assemblies. However, grassroots activists who volunteered as Babels found themselves in the difficult position of the *disruptive third* – i.e., in the role of communicative intermediaries between facilitators and other participants, collectively trying to enhance mutual understanding by attesting to imbalances of power and by challenging practices that marginalized some participants. The translators who occupied this role intervened between professional activists and other participants, thus becoming acutely aware of two opposing political mindsets: on the one hand, translators assisted in a process where facilitators felt an urgent need for timely decision-making, for "getting things done," in order to negotiate consensus within an extremely limited time-period; on the other hand, translators were required to listen to the sentiments of deep frustration, anger, and indignation felt by the majority of participants, many of whom belonged to grassroots global justice organizations, whose demands were systematically rejected when they did not fit the interests of the facilitators' group affiliations.

At the start of the European preparatory assembly that I attended in Paris, the Babels invited participants to hand over their passports as a deposit for a digital radio that would transmit simultaneous interpretation in at least six different languages. While they provided their services for free, they received modest ESF funding that covered this translation equipment as well as travel tickets to the European assemblies.

The Babels' new role distinguished them from other grassroots participants in a vital way: they were required to avoid taking stances on issues, and instead to listen thoroughly to all of the parties involved. This enabled them to become witnesses to patterns of inequitable practices that were taking place during high-stakes decision-making in the European plenary assembly – which created a dilemma for them.

---

[3] All names used are pseudonyms to provide anonymity.
[4] Interview with a Babels founding member, conducted in Vienna, January 8, 2006.

While the Babels' service as perceived technical translators placed them at the heart of decision-making, it also confined them to a marginal, rather non-participatory role. Treated by ESF facilitators as mere "technical service providers," the Babels saw their inclusive interpretation and translation practice as essential to democracy within international meetings (Boéri and Hodkinson 2004). Their dissatisfaction with the position imposed on them by the facilitators provoked them to find ways to intervene publicly on behalf of disempowered groups – that is, to serve as political translators taking a new and visible role.

THE STUDY: COMPARING DELIBERATION IN MULTILINGUAL AND MONOLINGUAL ESF MEETINGS

To understand both the impact and the limitations of political translation in the ESF, this study compares deliberative decision-making as practiced in the multilingual European preparatory meetings with deliberative decision-making within national preparatory meetings. Each meeting I studied involved one hundred to four hundred participants, taking place between 2003 and 2006. My ethnographic comparison analyzes the contextual conditions of transnational deliberation by focusing on questions of inclusiveness and transparency. Inclusiveness, first and foremost, is central to what defines grassroots democracy and deliberation in social movements (della Porta 2005a; Smith et al. 2007; Young 1996). Second, given the financial and logistical challenges ordinary citizens and grassroots activists face in their attempts to attend public forums that are not located in their home countries, inclusiveness and transparency become even more critical in deliberation conducted in transnational public arenas (della Porta 2005a; Fraser 2007; Lang 2013). I attended a total of nine national meetings and eleven European assemblies, which together constituted nearly half of all of the meetings that occurred during the period I analyzed. Both European and national ESF preparatory meetings worked with the same radical democratic principles for consensus-based decision-making inspired by the World Social Forum Charter of Principles (WSF 2001).

Because I was interested in the challenges that can be encountered in the process of democratic deliberation, I selected three different national Social Forum assemblies, which together provided an array of different conditions affecting the level of inclusiveness in a given deliberation. I selected the British national ESF preparatory meetings as a case that would be less likely to display inclusive deliberation given participants' perception of deep cleavages within the domestic arena of global justice activism (Maeckelbergh 2004). In contrast, I expected the Italian national Social Forum process to provide a case for more inclusive deliberation based on reported perceptions of positive cooperation and trusting relations among radical movements, NGOs, unions and political parties (della Porta and Mosca 2007). I also anticipated that the German national preparatory meetings would foster a cooperative practice of deliberation given that many participants acknowledged perceiving fewer preexisting conflicts than existed in other national Social Forum processes (Doerr 2009).

My comparative method combined three different approaches to understand social interactions and deliberation taking place in the meetings I analyzed. First, I worked as a participant observer, transcribing and analyzing deliberative decision-making in the meetings that I attended. During multilingual European assemblies, I tape-recorded and transcribed plenary discussions in the speakers' original languages. I speak German, English, French, Italian, and Spanish. When Hungarian-, Russian-, Turkish-, Kurdish-, or Greek-speaking activists spoke within an assembly, I was not able to understand them and relied on the simultaneous interpretation by the Babels. My analysis focused mainly on decisions made during public plenary sessions.

Second, working with qualitative semistructured interviews and a survey, I analyzed participants' *perceptions* of the quality of discursive decision-making in meetings. I conducted multiple rounds of qualitative, in-depth interviews before and after each European and national preparatory meeting. I interviewed eighty participants in all: fifty involved in the various national preparatory meetings I studied and thirty involved in the European assemblies. I balanced my sample to reflect activists' diversity in terms of political orientation, organizational background, gender, nationality, time of participation, and age.

Third, I did a survey ($N = 100$) to refine the hypotheses gained through my previous interviews. In the survey as in the interviews, I asked participants to compare the European and national meetings they attended, based upon: (1) how *transparent* they perceived meetings to be; (2) the availability of *opportunities for all participants to make a statement*; (3) their perceptions of *facilitators' attentiveness*; and (4) their impressions of the quality of *equality* and *inclusivity* within decision-making.

Comparative Focus: Co-decision-making between National and European Meetings

In order to compare deliberations that took place in European assemblies and national preparatory meetings, I focus on key issues that were addressed in both types of meetings and that involved similar conflicts along similar party lines. For many activists participating in the European assembly in Paris 2003, the aforementioned conflict over the distribution of seats for speakers for the upcoming ESF summit was one of the most contentious battles. Co-decision-making involved, first, an initial step during national preparatory meetings, which included different political factions. This was followed by a final decision-making process, which occurred at the European assemblies and included groups from each country.

In the three-year period in which I studied deliberation at ESF preparatory assemblies, I traced the co-decision process regarding the national lists of speakers, which was, in fact, one of the most politically influential decisions made regularly at both the European and national levels. Conflict over how to distribute the available number of seats among a large number of stakeholders and countries also symbolized the greater problem of equality in a European community of cooperation – something that European social movements were fighting for in a much broader context. While seemingly a banal organizational decision, the deliberation about the speakers list was also, in my opinion, a test to see if the heterogeneous and still very nationally oriented social movement groups engaged in the ESF could cooperate democratically. As in the context of EU politics, the wealthier national delegations in the ESF did not want to share their seats or their financial resources for plenary speakers with poorer national delegations, and this led in multiple meetings to conflict, stalemate, and crisis.

A PUZZLING OUTCOME: MULTILINGUAL EUROPEAN MEETINGS WORK MORE DEMOCRATICALLY

Before looking at conflicts over power and influence at the European meetings, I needed to review deliberation and shared decision-making between groups taking part in national preparatory meetings. I had expected that grassroots activists would perceive the national-level meetings to be more democratic since they (a) were generally more easily accessible, geographically, than the European preparatory meetings and (b) were held in the home language. Instead, national-level meetings suffered from multiple democratic pitfalls and crises, primarily due to *positional* misunderstandings, as I will demonstrate for each of the three national cases of Social Forums studied. Here, I first present the results of a small survey of participants' perceptions regarding national meetings versus European assemblies.

Participants perceived European preparatory meetings to proceed in a more "inclusive" and "transparent" manner than preparatory meetings at the national level. The survey asked activists participating in both European and national preparatory meetings to compare their impressions of potential barriers to internal democracy at the two sets of meetings. I received a response rate of 70 to 80 percent for my questionnaires distributed in the European and respective national meetings in Germany, the United Kingdom, and Italy in 2003–2005. I found that the majority of participants who returned my surveys perceived discussions and decision-making in the European assemblies to be more inclusive, *dialogical*, and transparent than in national preparatory meetings. Overall, 66 percent of the respondents who participated in meetings at the European and national levels perceived decision-making in European assemblies to be more inclusive of all the voices present as compared to national meetings. Just over half of the respondents (59 percent) perceived decision-making in European assemblies to be more transparent than at the national level, while slightly more than a quarter (27 percent) were of the opposite opinion (see Table 1.1).

TABLE I.I. *Perceptions of Inclusiveness and Transparency in National-Level versus European Meetings*

	Inclusiveness (%)	Transparency (%)
Response options:	*At which layer of meetings did you perceive decision-making to be more inclusive?*	*At which layer of meetings did you perceive decision-making to be more transparent?*
Preparatory meetings at national level	24	27
European preparatory assemblies	66	59
No differences observable	10	14
Number of cases (N)	30	30

One must interpret this evidence prudently: First, my sample is much smaller than the actual number of participants in the European and national meetings. To tackle potential response bias in the surveys conducted, particularly regarding a possible lack of answers from activists who did not speak English, I (a) oversampled activists who did not speak English and (b) worked with translators to render the questions into a variety of other languages. However, even though I selected a sample that would reflect the participants' diversity, including national backgrounds, identities, and ideologies, the potential risk of nonresponse bias exists because the participants who potentially could respond to these comparative questions needed to have experience at both the national meetings and the European assemblies. Thus, the opinions of first-time participants, and of those who never had the opportunity to participate in both types of meetings, were not measured. A preliminary impression based on these findings is that a broad majority of the participants, nearly a third of those who had filled out my survey, perceived the European assemblies as more inclusionary and transparent arenas – the opposite of what most democratic theorists would have predicted given the multilingual character of these meetings.

NATIONAL ESF MEETINGS: POSITIONAL MISUNDERSTANDINGS IMPEDE INCLUSIVE DEBATE

In order to understand how and why participants were not included in decision-making at national preparatory meetings, I review three such national meeting arenas – in Germany, the United Kingdom, and Italy – focusing on facilitators' and participants' perceptions and the actions they took in order to expose inequity and marginalization during deliberation. I begin by comparing the views of individual participants and facilitators regarding interactions that took place at these at national-level meetings.

German Social Forum Meetings: Facilitators Marginalize Immigrants and Local Participants

Grassroots activists involved in national preparatory meetings in Germany perceived democratic deliberations there as lacking in transparency and inclusiveness. When it came to decision-making for their national list of speakers, for example, members of local Social Forums and participants from resource-poor local grassroots groups stated during interviews that facilitators did not take into consideration their proposed nominations for the ESF plenary meetings. Instead, the facilitators – national-level professional activists who came from leftist political parties and unions – imposed their own representatives as speakers.

One of the local activists who spoke of this issue in her interview was Samira, a social media activist who had migrated to Germany from the Middle East. Samira was an active member of a local Social Forum group in western Germany. She helped German Social Forum organizers mobilize immigrant networks to participate in the ESF. I met Samira when she was a participant at German national preparatory meetings in Frankfurt. German meetings were easy for Samira to attend, since she had lived in Germany for over two decades and was fluent in German as well as in her native language, Farsi. I had expected that the distant locations and linguistic barriers would make it extremely difficult for Samira and other immigrants to participate in the European preparatory meetings. However, Samira attended those meetings, and she observed that although she had had some communication difficulties due to linguistic issues, deliberation there felt more democratic to her and other grassroots participants than it did at the national-level meetings.

Samira worked in low-paid, temporary jobs and had less money than other participants in the national preparatory meetings, and she was explicit about the problems she experienced there as a result: "In the national meetings, we are treated as if we were air. They talk about us but not with us, even if we are there and sit in the same room as them. There is just no reaction concerning questions which we migrants consider to be important. At the European assembly in Berlin, there was a different atmosphere. Also in [the European meeting] in Florence."[5]

Samira's professed feeling of invisibility in national meetings – a reaction to facilitators' talking *about* immigrants rather than *with* them – reflects a *positional* misunderstanding between participants like herself and the high-ranking professional activists who were acting as supposedly neutral facilitators. Her sense of being "treated as if we were air" vividly illustrates the impact of marginalization on immigrant women by dint of their gender, ethnicity, and

[5] Interview conducted in Paris, September 29, 2003, in German. My translation into English.

group affiliation. Other grassroots activists whom I interviewed confirmed Samira's impressions of the difficulty of participation for immigrant women in particular. One said: "The meeting was dominated by a certain culture of discussion and a certain way of speaking ... When you wanted to ask the questions that matter, you got unclear answers. You were not allowed to ask the wrong thing. Our questions remained unanswered. They have still not understood that migrant women are part of society."[6]

As a participant observer, I attended the German national preparatory meetings in order to be able to compare the *perceived* experiences of interviewees with my own observations of the discursive interactions in the meetings. I noted that often when Samira and other German national grassroots activists attempted to offer proposals, the facilitators interrupted them. Other locally based grassroots participants also described this as a problem, mentioning that it affected not only immigrant women but also others. A German activist from the ATTAC network[7], a transnational organization concerned with regulating financial markets, described how a facilitator, a national leader of her group, not only interrupted immigrants but also silenced local grassroots activists and women like herself in other situations:

He always answers for other people even though he was not asked. I was asking questions and [he] just did not let the other person answer, manipulated everything. [He] can just take over everything. We, a part of the local grassroots participants who form part of the German ESF preparatory assemblies, don't want such power structures.[8]

In total, 70 percent of the participants in the national preparatory meetings whom I interviewed named a lack of transparency on the part of facilitators and other professional activists as the reason why their own demands were not considered within decision-making.

Complementing these impressions on the part of participants, I witnessed directly how the facilitators' position of power allowed them to purposefully neglect voices they did not want to hear. This had negative consequences for immigrants like Samira and other "locals" who had a political interest in proposing speakers for the ESF. For example, in one national preparatory meeting in Frankfurt, Samira demanded that immigrants, who made up a significant part of the German Social Forum, should be included in the official German national list of speakers who were to be invited to the ESF in Paris. The facilitator interrupted her, saying: "You are too late. The list has already been closed."[9] Another German leftist party organizer who was the host of the meeting

---

[6] Interview conducted in Frankfurt, September 29, 2003, in German. My translation into English.
[7] ATTAC stands for the Association pour la Taxation des Transactions financières et pour l'Action Citoyenne, a transnational global justice network. It was founded in France in 1999 for advancing the regulation of financial markets, and has chapters in Germany and many other European countries.
[8] Interview conducted in Paris, September 29, 2003.
[9] My fieldnotes. German national preparatory meeting, Frankfurt, September 3, 2003.

added: "There was an email where this was said, and a deadline. The email list is accessible to all and you should have made your demands on that list."[10] In justifying the rejection of Samira's claim, the facilitator and his colleague here used her noncompliance with procedural *validity criteria* (cf. Glaeser 2010). In other words, her point was *invalidated* – due to the claim that she had not complied with a deadline. However, in interviewing several other participants, I found that, contrary to the response given in public to Samira, the email list had not been open to the *local* grassroots participants who formed part of the national preparatory meeting but only to a self-selected group of "national coordinators" – a designation referring to professional activists who supported each other while meeting separately before the beginning of deliberation.

When I questioned the facilitator regarding the criticism posed by grassroots activists, he said: "All our meetings are open and transparent. It's true that one time a migrant wasn't put on the email list; that was a technical problem, we'll fix it."[11] This facilitator's comments make clear that professional activists and facilitators were cognitively able to understand the points made by those representing the grassroots base of the meeting; yet they did not effectively count those voices during deliberation and excluded them from decision-making. The facilitator's perception of the situation – as a one-time technical glitch leading to a single omission – contrasts dramatically with Samira's picture of systematic exclusion. In contrast with the facilitators' perceptions, my observation of GSF preparatory meetings document that (a) the official German national list of speakers under discussion did not include a single immigrant, and (b) facilitators systematically dismissed the concerns of grassroots participants expressed within national preparatory meetings. The fact that facilitators did not see these issues as problematic indicates a certain *preconscious* element: that is, facilitators did not seem to be entirely aware of the concerns raised by a number of other participants in meetings.

The preconscious nature of positional misunderstandings on the part of facilitators often concerned issues involving citizen equity. These problems did not arise from evil intent. Rather, professional activists associated with institutional leftist political parties and ATTAC, who facilitated all of the sessions of the German Social Forum preparatory assembly, saw themselves as benevolent experts: distinct from the local grassroots activists, yet legitimized to speak on their behalf in the European assemblies. In one interview, a facilitator said, "In European meetings, Rudolf and I represent the consensus of the German preparatory assembly."[12] Facilitators' presumptions about their own ability to represent others, accompanied by their unequal sharing of information, decreased the levels of transparency and inclusivity during national-level preparatory meetings.

[10] My fieldnotes. German national preparatory meeting, Frankfurt, September 3, 2003.
[11] Interview conducted in Frankfurt, September 3, 2003.
[12] Interview conducted in Frankfurt, September 3, 2003.

UK Social Forum: Organizers and Facilitators Marginalize
Anarchists and Local Participants

I expected participants from small, local Social Forum groups in the United Kingdom to have the most unfavorable view of democracy during deliberation at the multilingual European meetings, since many British Social Forum activists had complained about meetings being dominated by continental European parties and old leftist ideologies (Maeckelbergh 2004; Nuñes 2005). When I met Paul in 2003, he was a London student engaged in direct action with autonomous groups in his local community. When I interviewed Paul during the turbulent European preparatory assembly in Paris, his comparison of the various meetings he had attended surprised me:

If you ask about the atmosphere within the European assemblies, I have to say that the [British] national meetings are less democratic.[13]

His perception was typical of the majority of British participants interviewed across all of the various political affiliations represented in the UK Social Forum preparatory assembly. Grassroots activists – as well as those who were members of the dominant unions and political parties – consistently reported that they felt the European preparatory assemblies offered a more democratic arena than that of national preparatory meetings.

Positional misunderstandings in the British Social Forum stemmed from differences of ideology and class among the British global justice activists who were participating in these meetings. As with the German case, the British national Social Forum preparatory assembly was divided into two main camps. Professional activists representing leftist political microparties, such as the Socialist Workers Party (SWP), formed one coalition with large unions and NGOs (Doerr 2009; Rootes and Saunders 2007). The second camp comprised members of local Social Forum and "horizontal" groups, including participants who identified as environmentalists, feminists, and anarchists, as well as those who feared domination by professional groups. These groups used the term "horizontality" to express disapproval of hierarchical structures consistent with their preference for an egalitarian, grassroots democratic model of deliberation in the Social Forums (Juris 2005, 2008a; Maeckelberg 2004, 2009). Among all of the British interviewees, "horizontally oriented" activists, such as Paul, were the most pronounced in their general critique of facilitators and socialist and old leftist party officials present within national preparatory meetings. Paul said:

Public decision-making in the national preparatory meetings did not take place. There was a cultural clash between what I would call the real Social Forum people and the professional Old Left organizations that brought the ESF to London. The European level

---

[13] Interview conducted in Berlin, June 20, 2003.

is more complex, diversified, and in this sense more public. In the UK this has to do with internal cleavages.[14]

In keeping with the view of this as a case of positional misunderstanding, Paul described a "clash" between different groups and individuals at the British national preparatory meetings. What bothered him during national-level preparatory meetings was definitely not a lack of inclusivity in terms of national and ethnic diversity. In comparison to the German meetings that I attended, British national Social Forum facilitators worked hard to include immigrants and Muslims within their national list of speakers proposed for the ESF (Doerr 2011). Nevertheless, as Paul and other interviewees pointed out, the facilitators present at British national preparatory meetings who belonged to unions and socialist and Marxist parties entirely ignored participants from different political backgrounds (such as "horizontals").

As a result of this deep division, professional activists initially proposed a national list of speakers for the ESF in Paris that only included members of their own organizations – a scandal that local grassroots activists were only made aware of at the European preparatory assembly in Paris. True, the list included a few speakers with immigrant and Muslim backgrounds, but only those who were part of the dominant party organizations; no other groups were represented. As a consequence, local grassroots members of leftist parties criticized national leaders about their exclusionary leadership style. For example, a member of the Communist Party of Britain made a public speech in front of fellow European comrades in Paris to report on some of these internal problems with the UK Social Forum democratic process:

Until now we in Britain have not seen much of democracy and transparency. Now tell me, how can I trust these people?[15]

When I confronted British leftist professional activists, who worked as facilitators in the national preparatory meetings, with the critique expressed by the quoted speaker and other leftist allies, they admitted to having communication problems with other groups, particularly with horizontal groups. One of the facilitators explained why she ended up having increasingly difficulties in taking horizontally oriented activists such as Paul seriously:

Personally, the groups that call themselves horizontals behaved like children – how could we have trusted them? A part of the activists in the meetings behaved in an arrogant and upper-class manner. In one meeting, they behaved respectless [*sic*] towards the employees who served them with drinks – this was so ridiculous. They asked for money, but they did not represent anyone – why should unionists who spoke for many members give the money to them?[16]

---

[14] Interview with an activist from Indymedia, London, June 2, 2007.
[15] European assembly, Paris Bobigny, November 11, 2003.
[16] Interview with a member of the official preparatory group of the London ESF, London, May 20, 2007.

Clearly, positional misunderstandings worked in two ways: grassroots activists were not the only participants who perceived other factions' behavior as disrespectful. Socialist party members and unionists serving as facilitators also described such experiences, particularly in interactions with those who identified as "horizontals." The behavior this facilitator describes is not of the sort one would expect from self-professed horizontal activists. In the perception of this facilitator, the "horizontals" for whom egalitarianism is a supreme virtue and a point of pride behaved in an "arrogant and upper-class manner" toward party staff who served them during a meeting. As Betsy Leondar-Wright shows, socially disadvantaged groups and working-class people may experience interaction with upper-class participants during meetings as marginalizing, undermining the intention of those who try to build dialogue between different groups (Leondar-Wright 2014).

As with the case in Germany, positional misunderstandings between British facilitators who informally led the meetings and the grassroots activists in attendance generated systematic disagreement about all questions discussed, from the location of future meetings to timing and financing. But unlike in the German case, in the British case it was socialist facilitators, themselves professional activists, who felt insulted by local horizontally oriented activists and their an "upper-class" style. A failure of mutual recognition made for positional misunderstandings within two different national arenas.

In comparison to the German case, though, British national preparatory meetings took place in a more hostile atmosphere – a perceived "cultural clash," in which every statement, and also nonverbal interactions, could be easily misunderstood by members of different groups. However, it was also clear that facilitators held the power. For example, at one of the British national Social Forum preparatory meetings I attended, local Social Forum members from Paul's group attempted to allow all participants to sit in a circle. However, on the next day of the meeting, professional activists had reordered the chairs in a style to which they were accustomed, a stage/audience setup in which the separation between facilitator and participants was more pronounced. In another striking example, the national list of speakers proposed by the British Social Forum to the European assembly included only members of the national board of the SWP, a move that was attacked by other local and subnational boards of the party.

Italian Social Forum: Facilitators' Personal Preferences and Unintended Marginalization

As in the UK and German cases, but to an even greater degree, I expected participants from local Social Forum groups in Italy, such as my interviewee Giulia, to have a positive view of their national Social Forum preparatory meetings' democratic process. Giulia had cofounded one of the earliest Social Forums in Europe, the Genoa Social Forum, and had participated in many of the European preparatory meetings over the years. Yet this longtime Italian organizer felt frustrated about her national delegation's informal preparatory meetings. Having formed close relations with each other, professional activists at the meetings in Italy were perceived as talking exclusively with delegates from the largest national organizations, while neglecting voices from local Social Forums and more "radical" groups. In Giulia's words:

Also in Italy, ... it is always the same people who "decide": only bureaucrats who hold positions in organizations and tend to prefer talking amongst themselves and not with people who do not speak for a big organization.[17]

Giulia describes the frustration she and others felt with an increasingly exclusive culture of political debate among professional leaders in Italian national preparatory meetings, which implicitly or explicitly marginalized the local groups who had actually initiated the Social Forums in Italy. The impressions conveyed by grassroots interviewees like Giulia surprised me, partly because many of them had been founding members of local forums, but also because the facilitators of the Italian national preparatory meetings, in contrast to those in Germany or the United Kingdom, seemed to have experience as mediators and to be putting great effort into being inclusive at the assemblies that I attended. A group of unionists and leftist party organizers, the facilitators at the Italian national meetings saw themselves as true *mediators*, translating between local autonomous, feminist, and national-level organized unions and political parties. One of them stated:

Inclusion is work. We organized many common meetings, and all of the spokespersons made an effort in order not to push their own groups' weight. Mediation is a political fact.[18]

Egalitarian facilitators in Italy, such as this interviewee, exerted considerable effort to include everyone in the discussions, using skills they described as being based in feminist consensus decision-making. Unlike their German and British counterparts, these organizers worked intentionally to include local and different ideological groups. Why then did some Italian grassroots activists feel that the leaders talked only among themselves?

In comparison to the British and German national preparatory meetings, Italian preparatory meetings that I attended featured a dialogical atmosphere – reflecting facilitators' efforts, about which they spoke in interviews, to be inclusive. While this effort matched the facilitators' perceptions of their own monitoring of the deliberations, I noticed other conditions that dissatisfied participants. In one situation, unionists who were acting as facilitators seemingly unintentionally favored certain participants over others. "Ah, here

[17] Interview with an activist from the Genoa Social Forum participating in the ESF 2006 in Athens, conducted in Athens, May 7, 2006.
[18] Interview with an international secretary from the FIOM-CGIL union, conducted in Florence, February 20, 2006.

comes Gigi from Milan," noted a facilitator in one assembly in Rome.[19] All meeting participants had been personally invited by email, but unionists who were well-positioned in close personal and professional relationships with facilitators quickly dominated discussions, as did professional activist Gigi, who showed up late to the meeting but eventually dominated the discussion with lengthy statements, leaving little space for grassroots activists to intervene. A grassroots activist from an anarchist group commented, "These people know each other since years, and some will receive more attention than others in decision-making."[20]

The Italian case not only suggests that positional misunderstandings divide groups along lines of identity and ideological differences, as in the two other national cases, but also highlights one of the most intriguing findings regarding "neutral facilitation" and democratic deliberation: personal relationships can unwittingly distort democratic deliberation, even when, as in this case, facilitators make an effort to work with a feminist consensus model in hopes of including all participants equally (Freeman 1972). Whatever their egalitarian ideals or intentions, people naturally tend to acknowledge and associate most readily with those with whom they already have familiarity, friendly connections, or established community ties (Polletta 2002).

In addition, the Italian case confirms that positional misunderstandings are often preconscious in nature. All of the facilitators interviewed across countries and groups seemed unaware of the ways in which they were contributing to grassroots activists' indignation over feeling misunderstood or discounted during meetings. It is also important to note that grassroots activists were unaware of the ways they themselves sometimes discounted others' perspectives or of the fact that their communication style sometimes caused misunderstandings based on cultural distinctions. The important difference is that facilitators and professional activists held the power in national preparatory meetings, and thus they were in the position to dominate decision-making.

Summary: National-Level ESF Decision-Making Fails to Be Inclusive

As shown in the cases of these three national Social Forums, structural inequality can generate various types of positional misunderstandings that affect decision-making. At the heart of positional misunderstandings were not only perceptions of difference in identity and/or ideology but also structural differences in status and asymmetric access to resources and information. For each of the three national cases, my fieldnotes and interviews reflect biased decision-making outcomes concerning the national lists of speakers. As presented at the start of the European assembly in Paris (which would ratify each national list), the German Social Forum's national list of speakers, supposedly agreed upon by informal consensus at the national meeting, did

---

[19] My fieldnotes.   [20] Interview conducted in Florence, November 8, 2005.

not include a single immigrant speaker; the British Social Forum list included socialist and Marxist party members but excluded "horizontals" and local Social Forum members; and the Italian Social Forum list marginalized grassroots participants, especially women, despite requests by local feminist activists to alter these decisions.

MULTILINGUAL ESF MEETINGS AND NEW POSITION OF THE DISRUPTIVE THIRD

I had assumed that linguistic differences and considerable cultural misunderstandings would worsen power asymmetries and related positional misunderstandings during the European assemblies, the highest decision-making body of the ESF. And in fact, when I arrived in Paris for the major ESF European assembly, this appeared to be the case. I attended both the European and national meetings that co-decided the lists of speakers. At the European assemblies, positional misunderstandings and marginalization created an even more divisive setting than those I had observed at national meetings. However, while the conditions contributing to this division remained hidden and unresolved at national meetings, the misunderstandings and inequalities in the deliberation process at the European assembly were witnessed and eventually challenged by the translators.

As was the case in national meetings, the negotiations regarding the national speaker lists, in which a small number of seats were to be distributed among a high number of organizations across countries, were a highly contentious issue. Thus, I did not expect each of the national list decisions to be reversed at the European level, yet this is exactly what happened. At the European assembly in Paris, grassroots activists were able to negotiate changes in the decision-making process, reversing previous decisions made by Social Forum elites at the national level. In the case of Germany, for example, the large national social movement organizations and unions unexpectedly changed their previous decision in order to offer two of their own groups' seats to other groups whom they had tended to marginalize during the earlier decision-making. Likewise, the Italian movement leaders increased the proportion of women speakers in their national list to 50 percent. Even the hegemonic British SWP reluctantly agreed to include two speakers from antagonistic local groups within the British list. Table 1.2 gives an overview of these unexpected changes in decision-making.

The results reflected in Table 1.2 are particularly relevant when you consider that European meetings were multilingual arenas. The perception that multilingual and transnational meetings could be more inclusive and transparent than the national-level preparatory meetings goes against what theorists have previously argued. I expected deliberation at the European assemblies to face challenges as a result of both the high stakes involved and the intersecting linguistic and positional potential misunderstandings. However, the

TABLE 1.2. *(September 30, Paris) Results regarding the National Speaker Lists*

	Speaker list from Germany	Speaker list from Italy	Speaker list from the United Kingdom
Total number of proposed speakers	22	25	10
Groups who felt they were not fairly represented on speaker lists created at national-level meetings	Immigrants; local Social Forum groups	Feminists; anarchists; autonomous groups	Local grassroots members; "horizontals"
Changes made during European assemblies	Inclusion of several immigrants as proposed speakers	Gender equality (50% women) in selection of proposed speakers	Increased diversity in proposed speakers; inclusion of local Social Forum members and others previously excluded

Numbers based on my fieldnotes.

international meetings required the assistance of volunteer translators to overcome language differences. In the following analysis, I explore how the locally based grassroots groups whose proposals had been marginalized at national-level meetings were able to effectively push through their demands at the European level. I will discuss the conditions of political translation and other contextual aspects that contributed to this outcome.

I consider closely the conditions affecting deliberation at the European assembly in Paris because it was the most decisive meeting on the ESF's calendar in making a final decision about the national lists of speakers.[21] First, I examine translators' and facilitators' distinct perspectives to better understand how linguistic and cultural differences affected their work and why participants continued to experience marginalization. Then, through a focus on the decision-making process regarding the speaker lists, I examine the experiences of grassroots participants who persisted in trying to achieve representation despite facing numerous roadblocks, and I show how linguistic

---

[21] The Paris European assembly on September 29–30, 2003, taking place two months before the planned ESF in November 2003, which was the last venue for participants to ask for changes in the national lists of speakers.

translators supported marginalized participants by taking on the role of political translators to make positional misunderstandings more visible and to require powerful participants to listen and respond to others. Finally, I describe how the Babels' intervention ultimately led to inclusive decision-making during the European meetings.

The European Assemblies: Linguistic Translators Witness Marginalizing Facilitation Practices

Before attending the European assembly in Paris, the grassroots activists I interviewed expressed hope that domination by members of certain groups could be curtailed at the European assembly. The activists suggested that the presence of the Babels would make a difference. Paul, the horizontal grassroots activist from the United Kingdom, told me: "Babels' translation reduces the hegemony of those who have taken part for a long time. This makes access easier for newcomers."[22] I was at first puzzled by these impressions. During my own participant observation, I initially considered the Babels a relatively unspectacular and powerless group of unpaid voluntary translators, who seemed, however, to be viewed favorably by most of the nonleader meeting participants. Thus, it was initially unclear why grassroots activists felt translation by the Babels had the potential to break down the "hegemony" of organizational insiders.

The first day in Paris failed to open my eyes. At day's end a facilitator offered a rare expression of appreciation for the Babel's linguistic translation services: "And now, ladies and gentlemen, we want to all clap our hands to thank the Babels for their work." This benevolent yet limited gesture reflected the facilitators' general tendency, and indeed my own tendency at that point, to ignore the transformative role beyond linguistic translation that the Babels played in setting up the European assemblies. Indeed, even after the translators had demonstrated their political efficacy in a new role that they themselves had created, the Babels members still perceived that the European facilitators maintained the same distorted perception of and asymmetric relationship with them that they had experienced as grassroots participants at the national meetings: "We are basically like the service woman who brings coffee," said Arnaud, one of the translators at the Paris assembly. Another Babels volunteer, who translated French into Arabic and Turkish, described the Babels in this way:

What hurts the activist core of Babels is the general misunderstanding that we are a service provider, as if we were paid for what we do. Our primary wish is that everyone can express himself in his own language. Second, we want to help people who have linguistic capacities to develop their skills. So we function in a completely different manner than most ESF leaders believe.[23]

[22] Interview conducted in Berlin, June 20, 2004.
[23] Interview conducted in Berlin, January 30, 2010.

I first became aware of the Babels' critical role and their collective motivation to challenge inequality during meetings where I interviewed Babels members themselves. Through their growing experience as translating listeners, Babels members had begun to recognize how power asymmetries influenced the degree to which participants, particularly facilitators and those with more power, listened or responded to others' concerns. Their early role as ESF participant volunteers provided them with a unique perspective. As paradigmatic invisible translators, the Babels had the opportunity to witness the inequality that was at the heart of the political conflict occurring at the European assembly – yet their officially impartial role prohibited them from taking a stance. From this tense position of providing translation while witnessing positional misunderstandings, the translators – activists themselves – became concerned that the setting was making them accomplices in maintaining the very power asymmetries they wanted to contest. It appeared to them that facilitators were making decisions that reflected only the positions of the politically influential parties and unions with which they were affiliated. Arnaud expressed his frustration this way: "The forum is ruled by just a small, transnational, elite group of people. The facilitators in the European meetings, the French and the Italians, they have the power. In France, they are the ones who chair national preparatory meetings as well."[24] So translators decided to act.

Cultural and Linguistic Differences Challenge the Neutral Facilitation Model

The facilitators at the European meetings were typically professional party organizers and unionists who had been facilitators in national meetings – the same facilitators who, I had noticed, had failed to take grassroots activists' positions seriously. Since many Babels translators were known to be grassroots activists, many of these European assembly facilitators also held a critical view of the Babels' translation service. Despite these misgivings, however, the facilitators' political parties and unions, which funded the European meetings, did not think they could afford to pay for professional interpretation. Thus, many facilitators saw it as a necessary evil to work with volunteers who provided their linguistic service for free, receiving only minimal funding for simultaneous interpretation equipment and travel expenses. At times the facilitators saw the lack of a team consisting uniquely of paid professional simultaneous interpreters as a liability. A Greek leftist party member who for the first time was facilitating one of the European assemblies told me:

I was part of [one meeting in which] Babels tested the new digital simultaneous interpretation technology, but it completely broke down. I couldn't understand anything! I was really frustrated and wanted my money back. Technical questions regarding simultaneous interpretation are really not easy … Sometimes I honestly have the

[24] Interview with a Babels founding member, conducted in Vienna, January 8, 2006.

impression that people don't understand what I say and this is a big problem. My solution is to repeat what I want to say in English over and over again until they understand.[25]

Newcomers like this facilitator saw the Babels solely as a team of amateurs doing "technical" work. As his words attest, on one occasion, the Babels' simultaneous interpretation had not worked; and from the perspective of a professional activist, this facilitator attributed this technical problem to a failure and lack of professionality on the part of the Babels themselves. For many grassroots participants, though, linguistic exclusion from supposedly democratic proceedings was nothing new. There is some irony in the irate reaction of facilitators at the European assemblies who were newly experiencing the frustration of not being heard/understood by others: a condition that grassroots activists at the national level – many of whom were now Babels translators at the European level – knew well. Given the difficulties in communication, this facilitator and others were compelled to recognize the need to change their communication style in order to be understood by others. In some cases, as above, facilitators attempted to translate their own statements into English and repeated them until participants nodded their heads, a frustrating effort that revealed how much they wanted to make sure all participants understood what they were saying.

At first I interpreted facilitators' experiences, like those of the Greek leftist party member quoted above, as possibly opening them up to creating democratic changes in the decision-making process at the European assemblies. I thought that a growing awareness of cultural misunderstandings might enable facilitators to avoid the positional misunderstandings that derived from their own greater power. To understand whether or not this might be the case, I interviewed several of the more experienced facilitators who had attended other European assemblies, often as mediators within their affiliated national Social Forum groups. While these leaders *thought* that the diversity of the group and complexity of the issues they were discussing at the European level *demanded* a culture of mutual understanding for deliberations to make progress, my own observations do not confirm their impression that it actually did *generate* that culture. For example, a French unionist I interviewed who had worked as a facilitator in more than ten European preparatory meetings said:

One has to be honest: the Poles were not particularly present in the anti-neoliberal campaign about the European Commission's Bolkestein Directive [*a directive aimed at liberalizing services in the European Union*]. But they did not destroy the consensus – they understood us. We wanted to instigate a European struggle for [*to address*] climate change, but for them that meant the closure of factories, unemployment, which we do understand. If a firm closes, then it is always entire villages that become unemployed.

[25] Interview with a Greek facilitator, Istanbul, September 24, 2005.

These are always very complicated discussions; thus, mutual understanding is necessary.[26]

High-profile Western European movement leaders like this one wanted very much to be understood by and to understand their Central Eastern European colleagues. I found, however, that these facilitators felt mutual understanding and empathy primarily toward their leadership peers – that is, toward professional activists representing leftist parties and unions for each country. Without additional interventions by the Babels translators, the facilitators' desire for mutual understanding did not in fact facilitate the inclusion of the Eastern European groups in decision-making. For example, in several of the European preparatory meetings I attended, leaders from the powerful French and German national delegations expressed their pleasure that "the Poles" understood them. However, at the Paris meeting, these same powerful Western European organizations were unwilling to share resources with Eastern Europeans when it came to deciding on the number of chairs for speakers for Eastern Europeans at the ESF summit.

This contrast between the facilitators' perceptions of their own leadership and their actual decision-making behavior is exemplified by their failure to take seriously the demands made by grassroots activists – the Central Eastern Europeans in particular. Thus, even though conditions at the European assemblies contributed to an expectation that the movement leaders would handle deliberations with greater inclusivity, in practice they generally failed to do so. While the diverse conditions should have fostered an inclusive interaction style at European meetings, the uncertainty and complexity present in these settings also worked against the same groups that had felt marginalized at national meetings. It was in response to this continuing inequality that a group of seemingly inconsequential translators stepped forward.

Political Translation Lifts the Voices of Marginalized Participants during Decision-Making

To gain a clearer picture of how the Babels supported grassroots activists in achieving meaningful participation in deliberation at the European assembly, this section traces the decisions regarding national speaker lists that were ratified or co-decided at the European assembly in Paris. I examine the way in which translators transformed their roles during this process to address positional misunderstandings and support grassroots participants, resulting ultimately in changed deliberation outcomes.

Hours before the official plenary discussion was to begin, contentious debates about the lists of speakers took place among the more powerful groups in attendance. In each of the national Social Forum meetings reviewed

[26] Interview conducted with a French facilitator, Berlin, January 30, 2009.

above – in Germany, the United Kingdom, and Italy – grassroots activist members perceived the decision-making process and decision outcomes on the lists as unfair. Although grassroots activists came to the European assembly hopeful that their voices would finally be heard, they initially faced marginalizing practices similar to those they had experienced in their national meetings. The local French team of facilitators chairing the Paris meeting had fiercely defended the "French" consensus proposal on the list after challenges were presented by professional activists from other national delegations, notably the British, the Italians, and the Germans. Sounding apprehensive, the French facilitator thus opened the plenary discussion with the following words:

> Dear friends and comrades, the French delegation together with the Italian delegation has proposed the following list of national delegations as speakers for the plenary assemblies in the ESF. Note that this consensus proposal can hardly be changed because it is based on the consensus of each of the national delegations. In particular, the French national delegation will be unable to change its proposal.[27]

Samira, the grassroots activist from Germany, whom I quoted in my discussion of the German national preparatory meeting, had confided her hope of being able to change the German list at the European level. At the Paris meeting she advanced a public challenge and a private one. Samira's persistence in the exchanges reproduced below impressed me, given the ways I had seen facilitators ignoring or dismissing grassroots activists' input in the national meetings. After the end of the morning session of the Paris meeting, she described the experience this way:

> During a coffee break I tried to ask one of the [French facilitators of the European assembly] a question [concerning the inclusion of migrant speakers on the German list of speakers]. She replied that she unfortunately did not understand me as my English is very bad. So she went away to speak with another person and left me standing there alone.[28]

This moment highlights the ways linguistic *and* positional misunderstandings overlapped at European assemblies. In this off-the-record moment, Samira had tried to convince the French session facilitator, a unionist, to include at least one immigrant in the German list of speakers. Yet the facilitator would not listen to her in a situation where Samira apparently lacked the necessary foreign-language skills to make her point clear. Thus, Samira found that even informal opportunities for access were closed to her.

Still, Samira did not end her struggle for the inclusion of immigrant speakers on the German national list. After the coffee break, she went to the women's assembly that was hosted alongside the European assembly, and in that meeting loudly proclaimed her demands in a long speech outlining the marginalization she had experienced in both the national and European assemblies. She describes what happened this way:

[27] My fieldnotes.   [28] Interview, Paris, September 29, 2003.

In the women's assembly, I was furious. I spoke out about our situations as migrant women in Europe. Yet once again the French organizers of the women's assembly just nodded their heads. Apart from this they did not offer any reaction.[29]

As a participant observer, I had been present at that women's meeting. I had noted that, just as Samira reported, while she was delivering her speech in German, the facilitators, organizers from the World March of Women, "just nodded their heads," then spoke only French.

Unlike the French women, other grassroots participants in the European assembly *did* understand why Samira was so upset. Among them were Arnaud and others who had joined the Babels force of volunteers, themselves members of grassroots global justice organizations. Even Babels who were not themselves connected to grassroots organizations, a minority within the group, recognized the ways in which linguistic translation alone did not provide full access for all meeting participants. Emmanuel, a professional simultaneous interpreter from Paris who was also a member of the French facilitators' union, expressed frustration about how linguistic translation work at the European assembly often was ineffective in helping participants like Samira: "As translator, you are in a strange position: you have power and you don't have power."[30]

His statement alluded to the translators' power to support grassroots activist participants by listening to them, conveying their concerns to facilitators, and alerting facilitators when they appeared not to be listening to participants' concerns. For example, in one particular instance, taking advantage of his affiliation with the facilitators – fellow French unionists – Emmanuel attempted to persuade facilitators to interact more respectfully with foreigners and local grassroots activists. In an interview, he said:

I told [the French facilitator] that she should try to prevent the many small groups [from] feeling marginalized due to the arrogance of the bigger ones ... All they have to do is listen to each other and make concessions.[31]

Individually, however, these conversations did not seem to make a difference. The facilitators persisted in disregarding the demands of immigrants and other grassroots activists. Nevertheless, despite their prior experiences of disappointment on the national level, Samira and other grassroots participants from Germany persisted at the Paris talks in requesting that the German list include immigrants. When the participants repeated their request later at the official speaker-list discussion, they were again disregarded. It was then that the Babels, for the first time collectively, interrupted. Their spokesperson, Emmanuel, whom I had interviewed, protested against what the Babels perceived as domination on the part of leading organizations represented by the facilitator, and the Babels intervened by going on strike: "We translators now collectively interrupt our linguistic service."[32]

[29] Interview, Paris, September 29, 2003.   [30] Interview, Istanbul, September 24, 2005.
[31] Interview, Istanbul, September 24, 2005.   [32] My fieldnotes.

At this unexpected bombshell, the French facilitator at first looked irritated, then consulted with her Italian cofacilitator, and finally suggested a break. During the break, the German unionists and leftist party organizations consulted, in the end giving up two of their national-list seats to immigrants. Coming as an unexpected change from one of the most influential national delegations, this concession constituted a significant gain for local grassroots activists and immigrants from Germany. While the change was triggered by the Babels' efforts, it is important to recognize that political translation, beyond its direct impact on decision-making, inspired and socialized other low-status participants from different groups to raise their voices in solidarity with and support for each other. This became clear immediately following the Babels' strike, which lasted no longer than ten minutes, as facilitators quickly responded to claims being made. Through the exercise of both disruption and persuasion, by removing their translation activities temporarily and also simply by asking facilitators to respond to arguments made by less influential groups – such as immigrants', women's, and other grassroots organizations – political translators opened the door for members of these groups finally to be heard. And this dramatically changed the course of debate.

Meeting Participants Take Up Political Translation as a Tool for Democratic Access

During the ongoing debate about the speaker lists, the powerful effects of the Babels' strike continued to influence and inspire other participants to protest unfair decisions, in a context where the Babels continued to monitor the discussion. The process began with a Central Eastern European activist, Olga, making a timid demand that Eastern European women's groups who had no resources be invited to an upcoming ESF:

I am speaking on behalf of the Collective of Women in Eastern Europe. I want [to] point out a very sad issue that has occurred since the last European preparatory assembly. We proposed five women from Eastern Europe as speakers in the ESF and searched for funding for them to attend. Now I see none of them is on the list.[33]

The European assembly facilitator, a French unionist, answered:

To be honest, this is something that we will debate tomorrow afternoon as it concerns the [issue-specific] networks [*such as networks on women's issues*]. We have to deal with these concerns later.

Relying on what theorists call "procedural validity" criteria, the facilitator used the agenda to argue that issue-specific questions – such as those relating to women's networks – were not a legitimate topic in the debate concerning the national lists of speakers in the plenum. For hours, grassroots activists had been

---

[33] My fieldnotes.

complaining that facilitators prioritized some criteria, such as nationality, over others, such as gender, questioning the legitimacy of the consensus proposal, though the facilitator was unwilling to hear them.

Now, however, several people in different parts of the European assembly raised their voices on behalf of the Central Eastern European speaker, Olga, shouting in French and other languages toward the facilitator: "Let her speak!"[34] Annoyed, the facilitator retorted in English: "This is not the topic of debate!" "Oh yes, it is!" came the response from different sides. "Let her speak!"

At certain points, shouting spontaneously from the third section of seats, Italian feminists and other grassroots participants expressed their solidarity with Olga. At one point, a young local activist from France, a unionist like the facilitator, called out from her seat in French: "Couldn't the Italians renounce one of their speakers [on their national list]?" The facilitator bellowed back at her, in French: "They would never do that anyway."

The French facilitator knew how hard it had been to negotiate consensus with her Italian colleagues. She knew that Italian national delegates had been adamant about not changing the composition of their delegation. Her own national delegation from France therefore risked suffering a loss of speakers if more Eastern European women were to be included in the overall list of speakers. (Ultimately, the slots for speakers were to be distributed among all national delegations involved).

The Eastern European speaker, Olga, then intervened in English a second time: "OK, but ... I am very sad that Western Europeans have more speakers and these innovative women cannot attend." (Applause). A French unionist shouted in French from the assembly: "There are too many French speakers and too many men on all the assemblies!" The facilitator responded (in French): "It is clear that French women will stay. Italians, could you give up one of your speakers?" Now an Italian unionist stepped to the aid of her French colleague, approaching the microphone, speaking in English, to calm down the heated audience and justify her selection of speakers on the Italian list, which included more men than women: "Indeed, just to inform you: The speaker whom we had selected [for the specific plenary panel at stake] is actually a woman." The implied argument was that the national speaker lists need not be changed because in this case the Italian list included a woman.

A number of Italians in the front seats now jumped up and began a lively discussion with the Italian unionist and with each other, reflecting the pressure they felt to reconsider the gender composition of their national list. More and more participants questioned the underrepresentation of women on each list, and the discussion continued until the reluctant French facilitator, after conferring with her Italian colleague, conceded: "OK, OK, *d'accord*. We accept the proposed changes. Each time [and for each country] we selected one man and one woman for each topic and each plenary."

---

[34] My fieldnotes.

Surprisingly, by the time the facilitator made this announcement, dominant groups and organizations had already agreed about changing the composition of the lists in favor of gender equality, a change that the facilitator had previously perceived to be unthinkable. After their initial strike and during the entire discussion, members of Babels collective had combined subtle disruption and persuasion practices to support those voices whom the facilitator had previously ignored. For example, the Babels, who normally worked in boxes created for simultaneous interpretation, would occasionally intervene. Babels members had been visible in the assembly, monitoring the discussion and at times jumping in to ask facilitators to listen and be more inclusive of less influential groups, a point to which I shall return.

The facilitator had changed her consensus proposal, effectively granting the validity of points made by marginalized groups. A spokesperson from a small and resource-poor Eastern European women's group had been able to achieve not only the inclusion on the list of a speaker from her group but also an equal gender quota for all panels and countries. Later, I asked an Italian veteran feminist unionist about how feminists from her country managed to ensure that their demands were considered. She said: "In Italy, there has been a long fight to introduce feminist ideas, and it still goes on. In European meetings, we Italians learn to organize and structure ourselves."[35] Because of the dynamics influenced and monitored by the Babels collective, the Italian grassroots feminists had pushed through at an international meeting demands for gender equality that had failed at their national-level preparatory meetings. The Babels' intervention as a *disruptive third* voice inspired and encouraged in others a sense of agency, making it possible for different alienated individuals to imagine what Arendt terms a "power with," or, in other words, the capacity of different people to act collectively in public, reducing domination (Arendt 1958; Habermas 1977).

The young British local Social Forum activists and rank-and-file party members who had been marginalized in the UK preparatory meetings were also able to achieve inclusion at international meetings. An activist from Manchester, for example, initiated an open discussion in one European assembly in Genoa: "Why does the British list only include participants from England, and not from Scotland?" In Paris, another grassroots activist asked, "How is it possible that only members of the Socialist Workers Party are on this list and no local Social Forum members?" Following a contentious yet democratic public debate in Paris, the groups that had felt marginalized were able to gain concessions, including having their representatives as speakers on the British list.[36]

[35] Interview conducted in Florence, November 5, 2005.
[36] My fieldnotes, European preparatory assembly, Genoa, June 2003, and European preparatory assembly, Paris, November 2003.

To review the impact of political translation in the ESF, in the following section, first, I will discuss the conditions that contributed to the linguistic translators' successful political translation intervention. Next, I will discuss political translation as a strategy used by marginalized participants to support each other in having their voices included in decision-making. Finally, I will address potential power issues faced by the Babels.

DISCUSSION: POLITICAL TRANSLATION COMBINES DISRUPTION AND PERSUASION

The Babels had rescued the deliberations from the stalemate produced by overlapping positional and linguistic misunderstandings in the Paris assembly. The Babels' strike, however, was not as spontaneous as it seemed.

Several factors went into its planning and contributed to its success. First, the Babels member who announced the strike was a professional simultaneous interpreter and a loyal unionist whom the facilitators "trusted" more than other Babels volunteers. Second, any disruption in the linguistic translation service could bring the meeting to a halt; because of the high stakes involved in the political issues debated at the Paris assembly under enormous time pressure. This gave the Babels leverage to exert considerable force on facilitators to make concessions. Third, because the translators had preemptively built a mutual understanding regarding the forms of marginalization with which they had become familiar, they were able to act collectively and quickly. Fourth and finally, the Babels' continuing and varied uses of their position to communicate their concerns to facilitators seems to have had the cumulative effect of enhancing the facilitators' ability to understand, at the last minute, the marginalized participants' experiences of being discounted.

Given the entrenched nature of positional misunderstandings and privilege in the ESF meetings, the success of the interventions of the political translators depended on their ability to act as a collective. Individually, their influence would have been limited. Their interventions were effective because the translators combined the practices of disruption and persuasion. They disrupted the deliberative process only when they considered it unfair, at the same time persuading and teaching institutional elites how to democratize deliberation. The French facilitator who responded to grassroots activists' demands at the meeting described to me later how interacting with the translators transformed her own norms, as well as her relationships with the more marginal participants. In her analysis, "we" (her cohort of facilitators and professional activists) learned at that meeting:

In fact, Babels showed us how to build confidence, which is the most important thing. I like to call this method "baby steps." After [the Paris assembly], we fought for the inclusion of immigrant organizations in the ESF with a solidarity fund. At the European level, it helped us reach the most important European agreement ever, to defeat the European

Commission's proposal to liberalize services. I suspect that learning to accept our diversity is what allows us to continue working together following many moments of crisis.[37]

Political Translation Practices Transform and Strengthen
Deliberative Norms

Inspired by the Babels' struggle for political translation, at the Paris meeting, grassroots activists and other members who were not in leadership roles began to voice opposition to deliberation practices that they witnessed as being unfair. Members of different groups often found themselves in competition with each other to have their needs met in final decisions. At the moment when a facilitator interrupted a speaker, even when participants in the audience were not particularly sympathetic to the speaker's position, a critical mass of participants used the newly "open" space to question why speakers were not being given the opportunity to present their case. Once the translators' actions had brought into question the meeting's deliberative norms – by asking for all voices to be considered in decision-making and suggesting that no one should be interrupted when speaking – marginalized participants of all kinds supported one another in gaining access to the floor. This new dynamic ultimately caused facilitators to stop ignoring others' stances on important issues and to reconsider their proposals for decision-making.

In many ways, the achievement of political translation derived from the Babels' combination of both disrupting and intervening toward facilitators to persuade them to dare making more inclusive and fair decisions, a visible practice that would inspire and encourage a series of spontaneous interventions socializing a variety of low-status participants to support each other and dare disrupting unfair consensus practices collectively. Even though those participants intervened from a position that was not neutral, sometimes expressing themselves in highly emotional, nondeliberative ways, these disruptions led to a more inclusive democratic practice. In this highly asymmetric setting, the disruptive effects of political translation, the Babels' example and legitimation of critical interventions, and the Babels' continued informal interventions and monitoring of the debate had the result of countering the influence of the dominant groups, which the facilitators had implicitly protected, with the now newly protected influence of others.

The Babels and Power: Can Political Translators Avoid Becoming
Dominant Themselves?

Paul, the self-defined horizontal activist whom I had interviewed following the Paris meeting, was impressed by the Babels' performance at this international

---

[37] Interview conducted in Vienna, January 8, 2006.

meeting: "It is funny: Babels have a lot of influence on the elite in the European meetings, and I think they were at first not aware of this."[38] Later, Paul joined the Babels' volunteer force, using his skills as a media activist to provide free software for simultaneous interpretation equipment.[39] His joke highlights how the entry of new anarchist members further strengthened the Babels' capacity to plan critical and collective interventions within situations of domination: "When one of the dictators speaks, I will simply turn off the digital program. We can have twenty different languages, and it is all very economical . . . That's how we resist domination by a few in the forum."[40]

As new participants like Paul, with his decidedly subversive consciousness, entered the collective, the Babels had the potential to become a kind of new, hidden yet powerful protagonist. As political and linguistic translators who knew and understood more languages than most of the other participants, they could perhaps have ended up as even more powerful gatekeepers than the facilitators, influencing discussions toward their own interests when facilitation failed.

Yet in none of the meetings I attended was this the case: each of the Babels' interventions focused on member participation – for all, and not for any particular point of view. The Babels' practice of interrupting facilitators in a communicative way was also quickly adopted by many groups eager to prevent their own marginalization, inside and outside of meetings. And in some respects the Babels volunteers themselves remained as far from power as ever. Since the group's inception, they had typically found themselves at the bottom of the organizational hierarchy, treated as service providers by Social Forum elites – and they resented this. A grassroots unionist and Babels translator from Turkey told me: "As Babels we work under enormous pressure, and yet the meetings keep functioning. I'm very angry about [the ESF elites]."[41] This translator was identifying an ongoing tension and the failed recognition of ESF leaders of the relevance of the Babels network for democratic meetings. He was angry about how professional activists hosting an ESF event in Malmö, Sweden, in 2008, had refused to reimburse volunteer translators for their travel tickets. Even after the Babels took on their new, more visible role as political translators, the ESF financial decisions regarding linguistic translation did not improve, despite requests for better funding.

The Babels network of volunteer simultaneous interpreters was inspired by the idea of horizontal, egalitarian deliberation in multilingual meetings, in line with radical, consensus-based democracy (Boéri and Hodkinson 2004). The Babels worked together as equals. One Greek Babels volunteer described her

---

[38] Interview, Berlin, June 20, 2004.

[39] Nomad is part of the digital translation technology that the Babels activist interpreters developed for use in the Social Forums and in ESF preparatory assemblies. During the WSF and ESF organizing process, the Nomad project was designed in the spirit of "open software" to promote collaborative work and shared knowledge, and offered an alternative simultaneous interpretation system; see www.babels.org, accessed January 1, 2006.

[40] Interview, Berlin, June 20, 2004.   [41] Interview, Berlin, January 30, 2009.

first experience of staying with other Babels, who came from many different backgrounds and who were hosted at the same location during ESF summits: "This was the first time that I felt this solidarity, and it also created new relationships."[42] As opposed to fostering opposition, the entrance of new members – like Paul, who knew of problems specific to different national meetings – seemed to further enhance the normative, political orientation of transparency and radical democracy that characterized the Babels' work. For example, an immigrant who volunteered for the Babels network described instances in which she observed influential groups attempting to manipulate translation during European assemblies, something she had also experienced at national UK preparatory meetings:

I was among the voluntary translators from Babels. I remember one European meeting, which was particularly undemocratic. Political negotiation took place in small group meetings that worked partly without simultaneous interpretation, but as I am bilingual, I went to these meetings to make sure that the SWP [in the United Kingdom] does not abuse its power. A part of the English participants tried to trick the French and Italians by playing on subtle linguistic differences within decision-making. But as I speak both French and English, I told the French and the Italians what was going on and made sure that they knew that they were about to be manipulated.[43]

What distinguished the Babels from "neutral" facilitators was their unique position as a witnessing and disruptive *third*. Together, the insider knowledge of the Babels and their distinct communicative power as political translators allowed them to intervene in asymmetric conditions at European meetings in ways that no other mediator, facilitator, or group had been able to do. Despite their significant impact on the proceedings, the horizontal, network-like structure of the Babels and the lack of sufficient ESF funding produced a rotating member base and inadequate equipment supply, limiting their influence.

CONCLUSION

Theorists of culture, democracy, and political participation have noted the exclusionary character of political deliberation within multilingual and transnational political arenas, including those created by NGOs and social movement actors. From this perspective, the most surprising finding of my case study is that inclusive and transparent decision-making was better achieved in contexts with the greatest linguistic diversity – that is, within transnational, multilingual European assemblies – rather than within the more homogeneous and accessible national Social Forum meetings, as literature on democratic deliberation suggests (Archibugi 2005; Dryzek 2009). Facilitators in both the European assemblies and the national Social Forums failed to act as neutral intermediaries, a primary cause of the stalemate that led to the breakdown of

[42] Interview, Vienna, January 8, 2006.   [43] Interview, London, May 20, 2007.

national Social Forums. Focusing on the unique communicative power position of the Babels as a *disruptive third* actor democratizing ESF politics, I have shown how political parties and movement groups were able to overcome both stalemate and inequality during European Social Forum assemblies to enact a grassroots model of democracy.

Unlike other deliberation arenas that involve political actors or international institutions in which power differentials are quite obvious, the ESF involved social movement groups that, while having very different agendas, shared the desire to promote social and/or political equality. The ESF facilitators were individuals dedicated to raising the voices of others in varied political and social contexts, who saw themselves as inclusive of participants who held differing views. Their intentions notwithstanding, ESF facilitators contributed to marginalizing others in part *unintentionally* and *preconsciously* when facilitators themselves assumed positions of power. ESF facilitators' relatively privileged positions, intersecting with the dynamics of gender, class, and nationality or ethnicity, formed the basis of the positional misunderstandings that threatened stalemate in the future.

Unlike the facilitators, who reflected the interests of powerful, institutionalized groups to which they were connected, the Babels translators joined together to become an internally diverse network that reflected a combined knowledge that was inclusive and supportive of the varied ideologies held by the diverse identities represented in the Social Forum meetings. Collectively, they witnessed positional misunderstandings that occurred during deliberation and came to take on a new role as political translators – a role that enabled them not to promote an agenda but to support all participants having a voice. The translators' methods of political translation then became a model that members of groups could emulate in the interest of giving each other a voice in deliberation.

The Babels combined persuasion and disruption. Previous work has conceptualized activists as either contentious political actors who engage strategically and instrumentally within discursive arenas, or as deliberative advocates arguing on behalf of the common good (see, critically, Bob 2005). Rather than either originating or subverting deliberation, these activists, through their translation of the indignation felt by local participants, challenged the powerful to understand and engage in dialogue with disempowered groups.

The Babels' unique position as fair and reliable translators in high-stakes negotiations between factions gave them the informal power to (1) disrupt proceedings in order to require facilitators to listen to others and (2) communicate with facilitators to persuade them and other leaders to consider changing decisions that had been presented as final and unchangeable. This political translation counters the model of neutral facilitation advanced by many democratic theorists and practitioners of consensus-based, grassroots democracy.

First, it shows that in many settings, deliberative groups with only "neutral" facilitators tended to fail. Second, the political translators succeeded by acquiring both oppositional consciousness and effective political power through their insider-outsider positions. Third, three conditions made political translation effective: (1) a context of cultural and linguistic differences; (2) a commitment to equality among some privileged group members; and, (3) most importantly, the development of a disruptive third position by the translators.

In sum, the benefits of political translation extend far beyond linguistic or even cultural interpretation. The position of the disruptive third opens a new way to theorize democracy in social movements and their transnational communication and deliberation processes. In recognition of ways in which positional misunderstandings have impacted deliberative settings involving social movements, one could surmise that political translation could serve as a tool in other contexts where important decisions are made, particularly those involving institutional political actors or other settings where power differentials are more obvious. Chapter 4 will review ways in which grassroots community organizers in the United States have started applying political translation to challenge power asymmetries within local institutional political arenas involving working class residents, immigrants, and multiple language speakers.

Following my research in Europe, given that political translation allowed European assemblies to overcome internal crises and change deliberation practices that fostered a more democratic agenda, I considered a new question: could political translation also work in monolingual, national contexts, regardless of whether or not there was a need for linguistic translation? Chapter 2 will explore this question by focusing on the political translating work undertaken by young American grassroots global justice activists, many of them children of immigrants, who organized the first US Social Forum in a traditional monolingual American social movement context.

2

Frankfurt versus Atlanta

Political Translators as Coalition Leaders

The previous chapter documented how political translators at the Paris meeting of the European Social Forum (ESF) in 2003 helped steer participants toward more inclusive decisions in a transnational setting characterized by structural inequality. In Chapter 2, I look closely at the failure of neutral facilitation during Frankfurt's 2003 German Social Forum (GSF) meeting, whose facilitators struggled to achieve impartial conflict resolutions in a setting with intersecting gendered and ethnic boundaries (cf. Crenshaw 1989; Hill Collins 1998; Smith 2005; Roth 2003; Wood 2005; Snyder 2006; Yuval-Davis 2006; Marx Ferree 2009; Leondar-Wright 2014; Lépinard 2014). I then analyze a contrasting case in which, faced with the same problem in 2007, political translators in Atlanta produced a successful multiethnic coalition that would host the first nationwide United States Social Forum (USSF) event in the history of the United States. The USSF coalition, created around the same time as the GSF, succeeded in building two large grassroots face-to-face multiethnic deliberative forums on global justice, in Atlanta in 2007 and in Detroit involving almost twenty thousand participants in 2010. The Atlanta success derived from the emergence of a political translation collective in the United States, parallel to the Babels in Europe, following conflicts over race-based marginalization in the US global justice movement. The Atlanta political translation collective had no direct connections with the European Babels. Although the Atlanta team knew about the Babels' volunteer practice of language interpreting emanating from the World Social Forums, Atlanta founders traced their own intersectional translation practices back to the grassroots, US-based coalition of immigrants, language justice interpreters, LGBT organizers, and grassroots community educators working on antiracism and gender justice (cf. Klein 2010; Karides et al. 2010). This emergent collective of activists in the United States included many bilingual participants, immigrants, women of color, and LGBT activists who saw translation as a new paradigm for developing a more equitable model of internal democracy in American social movements. While the European Babels translators challenged inequalities in transnational, multilingual meetings, the US activist coalition of translators challenged racial and gender power asymmetries in the USSF national meetings.

The GSF coalition that met in Frankfurt provides a good case for comparison with the USSF because it struggled with two of the same internal conflicts. The GSF was hampered by misunderstandings related to culture, ethnicity, and gender, leading to the marginalization of minorities and immigrants. Conflicts over resource inequality and finances also split the resource-poor grassroots activists from the national institutional organizations that dominated the GSF coalition (Doerr 2007). Two years after the Frankfurt meeting that I describe, the GSF had lost 80 percent of its membership. In contrast, the USSF founders made it their primary goal to resolve conflict and misunderstanding between grassroots activists and professionalized NGOs and philanthropic foundations. While the GSF coalition failed, the USSF grew into one of the most culturally and socially heterogeneous face-to-face forums for civic deliberation in the United States (Smith et al. 2012).

FRANKFURT: THE FAILURE OF THE GSF COALITION

Founded in 2003, the GSF started as a pluralist and internally diversified national social movement coalition that initially included roughly seventy organizations and groups, about the same number that attended the initial national preparatory meetings at the Atlanta USSF.[1] GSF's founders included both a small number of affluent, national-level organizations and a multiplicity of spokespersons from resource-poor "local social forums" located all over Germany. The national-level organizations participating in GSF preparatory meetings included trade unions, such as IG Metall and Verdi; established transnational global justice networks, such as ATTAC;[2] and institutional Left foundations and political parties, such as the German Left Party. The local Social Forum organizers included anarchists, autonomous activists, feminists, environmentalists, and immigrants' rights activists (Doerr 2011), while also at times affiliating with institutional global justice networks, such as ATTAC.

Although the GSF began with considerable heterogeneity, coalition meetings following a nearly two-year period of successful meetings abruptly became more homogeneous in Spring of 2004, with many local Social Forum activists who felt marginalized choosing to cut ties with the coalition process. Ignorant of the causes and scope of this defection, GSF founders were unpleasantly surprised by the outcome of the planned 2005 national GSF summit. Organizers had counted on five thousand participants, but only about a

[1] These numbers are based on my interviews with GSF and USSF founders.
[2] ATTAC stands for the Association pour la Taxation des Transactions financières et pour l'Action Citoyenne, a transnational global justice network. It was founded in France in 1999 for advancing the establishment of a tax on foreign-exchange transactions, and has chapters in Germany and many other European countries.

thousand attended, most of them members of unions or the German Left Party. (Rucht et al. 2007). While the early national preparatory assemblies I attended had included a wide range of ideologies, identities, and age groups, including younger people in their thirties, the dozen participants in the last national preparatory meeting I attended in Germany before the summit were much older and more ideologically homogeneous, most of them belonging to the Left Party.

I quickly detected an undercurrent of conflict in the early GSF national preparatory meetings in 2003 and 2004. The facilitators in these meetings – all unionists, leftist party members, and academics who collectively shared a common linguistic and ethnic background – had difficulty understanding grassroots activists. This implicit conflict undermined their attempts at effective "impartial" conflict resolution. Also, although the GSF facilitators had intended to be inclusive of immigrants and minorities, they failed to recognize the need for special action in pursuit of that inclusion and the GSF's deliberation took place in a monolingual German-speaking setting. One typical GSF facilitator, Harald Kurtz,[3] was a professional activist working for the ATTAC network. Harald occupied the position of a founding member and informal leader. Officially, in accordance with the GSF's egalitarian model of consensus-based democracy, Harald also served as a neutral facilitator in the GSF national preparatory meetings. Yet his close connection to institutional organizations and his privileged if hidden leadership role made it hard for him to understand the experiences of grassroots activists, particularly those from resource-poor groups.

The first GSF preparatory meeting that I attended took place on September 13, 2003, in Frankfurt – a location chosen by Harald and his fellow organizers, who were leading unionists and Left Party organizers based in that city.[4] In the assembly itself, it did not take long for conflict to arise. By choosing Frankfurt, organizers had hoped to offer participants from all over the country a meeting space sponsored by one of the biggest unions. Yet neither the union nor the GSF had provided funds for grassroots or immigrant groups to travel to the city. Some of the grassroots activists therefore nurtured some grievances even before the assembly began.

At the beginning of the plenary session, I noticed that, as facilitator, Harald made a somewhat awkward effort to include ethnic minorities and grassroots activists – for example, by welcoming immigrant women as "guests," even though it turned out that some of them had already attended previous meetings. His unfortunate characterization implied that the women were less than full members. Trying to ascertain the causes for this behavior, I interviewed some of the facilitators at a later meeting. For Harald, the problem seemed to be that immigrant women failed to raise their voices within meetings, though he did not see this as a clear-cut matter of gendered marginalization:

---

[3] All names in this chapter have been changed.   [4] My fieldnotes.

With gender equality we do not have a problem here, I think. The women [at the Social Forum] are ... intelligent, like my daughter ... They know how to make a claim. I have a lot of respect for them. Here men, of course, take more space in the debates than women, because they are used to having more space, traditionally. And then, finally, one should not forget that there are still those [women] who don't speak up. They come, I suppose, rather from the Eastern countries and it might be more difficult for them; they are perhaps a bit shier.[5]

Harald's words illustrate a paradox: On the one hand, GSF facilitators such as Harald wanted to empower the perceived "shier" women as members of traditionally disadvantaged groups that were necessary for their coalition. At the same time, however, he implicitly saw immigrant and minority women as distinct from other women at the Social Forum whom he compared to "intelligent women, like my own daughter." Not recognizing these implicit distinctions, Harald saw "no problem" with gender equality in the meetings he cofacilitated.

The grassroots, and particularly the immigrant, activists in the GSF felt, to the contrary, that the facilitators disregarded their arguments. In one meeting in February 2004, for example, a Turkish second-generation immigrant in her thirties pointed to immigrants' and minorities' difficulties obtaining access to an ESF meeting that was to take place in London. This woman, who had residency in Germany but was not a German citizen, raised her hand and brought this issue to the facilitator's attention but felt rejected. When I interviewed her after the meeting, she reported her frustration with the facilitator, Harald:

My position has been pushed back from public debate with the justification that we don't have time for this right now. As an immigrant, I have, like many others, a big problem with London as the place where the next ESF shall take place. The probability that my visa request will be rejected is about 50 percent, because I cannot show to the English that I have work ... [Facilitators] do not like to bother with [this issue]. They believe that these are the problems of foreigners.[6]

This immigrant's impression overlaps both with my observations and with the transcript of discursive interactions in the meeting, here in the original German translated into English:

Extract from plenary discussion GSF prep. meeting, Feb 21–22, 2004

Harald, facilitator and professional activist: OK, we are pretty through with all the important stuff. So, since we have more time, the last point on the agenda is diverse issues. Everybody can bring up new issues they want to address now.

Linda, grassroots immigrants'-rights activist, working at the local level: Earlier today we have raised the problem for resident immigrants to get visa to participate to the ESF in London.

---

[5] My interview with a GSF facilitator, January 6, 2006, conducted in German, my translation into English.

[6] My interview with a GSF participant, February 21, 2004, conducted in German, my translation into English.

Harald: Of course, the idea about visa. Who else wants to talk about that subject?

Wolfgang, professional activist, unionist, and host of the Social Forum meeting: We've talked about it before; we do not need a public discussion about that now.

Harald: No public discussion. Good. Yes, I also agree that this issue has no place on our common public discussion agenda here today.

Wolfgang: I am satisfied if those who are affected by it will take care of visas themselves.

Harald: Yes, good. And we also have Linda, who has raised the issue so she can also take care of it. [*Linda protests in background.*]

Ayse, immigrant: I think that the question of visa does not only affect and concern immigrants!

Harald: Yes, that is clear.

Wolfgang (loud, annoyed): Good, but that is not something that we have to talk about now and here.

Neyla, immigrant: But don't you see how hard it is for many immigrants who live here in Germany to get a visa in order to be able to participate to the ESF in London, given the Schengen border regime and further EU regulations?

Wolfgang (loud, interrupts speaker): No, no, no. You don't understand. It is all different . . . If one is a German citizen one will not need a visa.

Hildegard, professional activist and member of the German Left Party: That is true. As German citizen one does not need a visa to travel to London.

Harald (calm): Exactly. Thank you, Hildegard. Good, so we continue. Let's talk now about the meeting of the Protestant Church in Germany.

After this, no other speaker intervened. Harald and the other professional activists representing institutional Left Party members and unions funding the GSF, remained calm and seemed not to notice the expressions of concern and dismay from the immigrant speakers (who had all been women). They went on with the discussion agenda on technical issues as if nothing had happened.

This interaction illustrates how GSF facilitators who genuinely saw themselves as empowering minority women in fact inadvertently marginalized them in the assembly. The gendered positions in this assembly were asymmetric: facilitators were mostly German men speaking from privileged and influential positions, occasionally asking a younger German female party colleague to cochair the meeting with them. Wolfgang, for example, an influential peace activist and Left Party member, was a member of the group hosting and sponsoring the location for the meetings.

In short, despite the self-definition of the Social Forum in Germany as a deliberative "open space," intersectional marginalization played a noticeable role in the dynamics. Neither the arguments made by the immigrant women nor their potentially important symbolic role exerted much impact on the decision-making. The facilitator, himself a professional activist, joined the position of the more privileged participants in the assembly, all of them professional activists, who supported each other while silencing and interrupting less privileged speakers. This example also indicates how facilitators who try to be neutral can fail to assume and hold a third position, by which I mean a position in between those represented by the parties in the room, intervening to promote deliberative equality. Without such a "third," good arguments may get lost in the process of being filtered through a "neutral" facilitator.

To fully understand how such positional misunderstandings increasingly divided grassroots participants and informal leaders in the GSF over a series of consecutive national preparatory meetings, we can explore the informal leaders' perceptions of themselves as neutral, impartial facilitators. For example, in his later interview with me, Harald explained his view of his "consensus" proposal not to talk about visa problems in the plenary assembly:

First, I think, the visa questions should not be discussed because we should wait to hear what [Social Forum organizers in] London say about this before we start a campaign. Maybe the English foreign minister will make an exception. Now we don't need public discussion about this. Maybe people could secretly "travel in other people's jacket pockets."[7]

Harald's suggestion that immigrants could "travel in other people's jacket pockets" references a popular German phrase poking fun at the illegal smuggling of undocumented persons across national borders. This rhetorical strategy unconsciously belittles the validity of the immigrant women's demand (Wodak 1998). The immigrant women were, unsurprisingly, the first group to leave the GSF coalition meetings.

So here we see the limits of a supposedly egalitarian model of facilitation that implicitly favored already-privileged national institutional actors and thus failed to translate to others the perspectives and arguments of local grassroots activists. From a strategic perspective, the case of the GSF also reveals a classical broker dilemma (Jasper 2006), as it was difficult for coalition movement leaders, such as Harald, to hold a neutral third position as facilitators while seated at the table with powerful unionists who were providing funding for the planned large-scale GSF event. (Andretta and Reiter 2009; Mosca 2007; Waterman 2004). The dilemma is compounded by silence surrounding questions of cultural diversity within mainstream German political discourse – a legacy, perhaps, of the World War II. Notions of race and ethnicity remain shrouded in taboo, associated as they are with guilt from Germany's history of racism, National Socialism, and the Holocaust (Olick and Levy 1998; Schwab 2010).

ATLANTA: TRANSLATING QUESTIONS OF DIVERSITY AND INEQUALITY

A passionate debate emerged over race in the summer of 2007 in Atlanta, Georgia, at the inaugural meeting of the USSF. The grassroots democratic USSF had brought together ten thousand participants from all over the United States; it sought to

---

[7] My interview with a GSF facilitator, February 21, 2004, conducted in German, my translation into English.

mobilize a national coalition to connect campaigns for global justice with domestic debates about immigration, race, and inequality. Building a successful coalition proved challenging. From the inception of the USSF kick-off meeting, immigrants, black community leaders, and grassroots global justice activists engaged in heated discussions with affluent philanthropic funders and representatives of established NGOs. After a plenary session on immigration reform, a white staffer from a large NGO concluded: "Grassroots activists who form part of the USSF care too much about racism and too little about policy. They are rigid, dogmatic, far from the world, and not concerned with having power."[8]

This was not the first time that internal conflict over race and power had divided Social Forum factions in the United States. In 2003 misunderstandings over racial issues and differences in regard to organizing internal leadership had undermined the first attempt to pull together a Social Forum event in the United States. This internal crisis put an end to incipient cooperation between the two camps: locally based, grassroots global justice groups dedicated to mobilizing immigrants, minorities, and poor people versus professionalized national NGOs and institutional funders (Karides et al. 2010; Smith et al. 2008). Scholars have interpreted such internal coalition conflicts in terms of market-based competition, with grassroots-activists' lack of resources forcing them to cooperate with professionalized, national-level NGOs and institutional sponsors (Guerrero 2008, 2010; Minkoff and Agnone 2010; Smith 2005). Although the professionalized organizations are necessary allies for social movements building national, policy-relevant coalitions, they also have the potential to undermine and coopt grassroots democratic processes (Meyer and Pullum 2015).

At this inaugural meeting in Atlanta in 2007 and in subsequent meetings, however, a critical third group intervened. The cultural intermediaries and linguistic translators who had participated in initial coalition meetings had witnessed the earlier misunderstandings over race and inequality. One of them described how he used to intervene between the opposing parties involved in the conflict over issues of race to reflect critically about their own statements toward other coalition members, saying, "The most important thing is always to slow down, taking the time, not making assumptions. [You have to ask participants who make potentially problematic assumptions] – what do you mean by this word, by 'it,' always getting the proper term."[9] In other words, these activists found it essential to urge participants to slow down, examine their statements, and consider their use of potentially stereotypical notions of other groups or participants.

The translators who intervened in Atlanta in 2007 were activists working for local grassroots organizations. Many were people of color, LGBT, or first- or second-generation immigrants (Guerrero 2008; Ponniah 2008; Karides et al.

---

[8] My interview, Detroit, June 22, 2010.
[9] My interview with a USSF organizer, Detroit, May 25, 2010.

2010; Smith et al. 2008). In an exceptional move, these few dozen organizers had brought together a new, nationwide Social Forum leadership that would avoid coalition breakup by placing marginalized populations at the center of decision-making. Jody Mayer[10] was among the group of USSF founders who fought to bring together the previously divided groups to form a new, national coalition. Jody was an experienced grassroots organizer, having worked with immigrants on the ground locally. Bilingual in Spanish and English, Jody had been a trusted presence in grassroots immigrant coalition meetings preceding the USSF event, providing linguistic translation for exchanges between local grassroots activists – many of them identified as people of color, Latino/as, and LGBT organizers – and English-speaking national NGO spokespersons and funders.

Jody's day-to-day work was for the Grassroots Global Justice Alliance, which connects national immigrant advocacy groups with grassroots social justice organizations throughout the United States. In this organization, Jody was accustomed to moving between languages and cultures, speaking English in national meetings and Spanish at local rallies. In USSF coalition meetings preparing for the event in Atlanta, she had often intervened when established NGO staffers working on immigration reform had trouble understanding not only the language but also the content and the importance of demands by undocumented immigrants. This work, in Jody's view, was political: it entailed "translating" into the language of privileged coalition members what daily racism meant for people of color in local communities. Jody explained when I interviewed her:

What we did for the US Social Forum was translation. For example, in the 2006 protests for immigration reform, millions of immigrants were on the streets; we needed to have these leaders at the forum. At the local level, our coalition is based on the work of young folks – many of them people of color, also queers. However, our national leadership in the US radical Left does not reflect that diversity. For us as Grassroots Global Justice Alliance, translation in organizing the first Social Forum in the United States [*Atlanta, in 2007*] meant, for sure, making a huge commitment to multilinguistic access. We translated the idea of a Social Forum to the US context. But it's not just about linguistic translation of documents and statements for immigrants and minorities. It's also about emotion. Translation means to bring in queer people, people of color. It's a translation of space, of class, of gender.[11]

Jody here defines translation in opposition to the conventional idea of "neutral" linguistic interpretation that transfers meaning from one language to another (Inghilleri 2012). The official ethics of linguistic translation hold that the translator or interpreter should make no judgments regarding differences of race, class, and gender. In contrast, Jody assumed that the *ideas* of race, class, and gender needed to be translated along with the language used to talk about

---

[10] All names have been changed.   [11] My interview, New York City, March 19, 2011.

them. In using translation in this unorthodox way, the new USSF leaders aimed to redefine the meaning of diversity within the coalition they were forming. The widespread perception of racial injustice implies a built-in justification for remediation, while class and gender inequalities, which also often distort communication, tend to be relatively invisible. Challenging the full range of inequalities meant fundamentally rethinking the way in which the coalition organized deliberation at its national meetings. This intersectional usage of the concept of translation was new in the world of American global justice organizing.

Ten years earlier, in the global justice mobilizations that began around the millennium, activists were already thinking about questions of internal democracy in social movements through the perspective of diversity and intersectional coalition work that addresses inequalities and boundaries of race/ethnicity, class, and gender (Roth 2003; Smith 2005; Snyder 2006; Marx Ferree 2009). Linguistic translators who formed part of the immigrants'-rights movement had seen themselves as "language justice" translators (Klein 2010). But unlike Jody, they had restricted their participation to the task of linguistically translating for others, consciously taking no active role within decision-making and leadership. Jody differed from these earlier translators in many ways. First, she held a leadership role in the coalition. Second, she used "translation" in an intersectional context to challenge inequality within the USSF coalition. She and other bilingual second-generation immigrants and people of color used their experiences as cultural intermediaries to rise to positions of national leadership, then leveraged their informal position of power to increase the stakes of minority groups and marginalized populations within the Social Forum.

In the USSF, as in the GSF, immigration was a hot topic during national planning meetings, dividing local grassroots activists and national-level professional activists working for NGOs and institutional organizations and funders. During USSF national planning, conflicts that arose over the inclusion of immigrants as leaders exemplify the witnessing position of political translators during preparations for the first national USSF meeting in Atlanta. An early institutional supporter of the USSF complained:

For the first USSF in Atlanta, [the issue was] proimmigration reform ... and it failed in Congress. And organizers in DC had worked their asses off while others had worked against it. Instead [of inviting those involved in working in favor of the reform], they devoted a plenary solely to those who had opposed it and then also had it be chaired by immigrants'-rights activists I had never heard about.[12]

Highly educated and trained professional staffers from NGOs, such as the interviewee quoted above, had worked exclusively with policy-makers and institutions in Washington, DC. They found it difficult to understand or even

---

[12] My interview, New York City, March 17, 2010.

talk with local grassroots organizers in Atlanta and in the US South. In this instance, grassroots immigrants'-rights activists on the national planning assembly had rejected the NGOs' demand to invite well-known institutional spokespersons close to the Democratic Party as keynote speakers for their first USSF event. This decision, which deeply upset NGOs working on immigration, reflected the ideological divide in the USSF and the cultural gap between the grassroots movement and the world of institutional NGOs. Much as in the GSF, the misunderstanding between the professional activists working at the capital and the local grassroots leaders was mutual.

In this increasingly tense situation, the political translators in the USSF reframed the conflict by intervening as a third, translating voice. As a USSF team member and political translator explained it to me:

Normally there would be someone standing in front of you and say[ing], "I don't like what you say." But with translation you don't have that confrontation. There is some-thing between. We call it "possession." This is one of the principles of language justice interpretation – that is, people advocate for themselves, to take ownership of your own liberation.[13]

This is a philosophy that emerged from the immigrants'- and civil rights groups that specialized in providing what they call "language justice interpretation" for linguistic minorities and immigrants at USSF events (Klein 2010; Tijerina 2009). The activists inspired and trained in this practice saw their intermediary role in meetings not as that of neutral facilitators but instead as protective advocates, allowing others to speak and "possess" the public space of meetings. Their ideology contributed to shaping the idea of political translation.

Political translation in Atlanta was also influenced by the experience of grassroots organizations on the ground who knew how to address issues of racial injustice and poverty in heterogeneous groups. Will Parker, the founder of the Atlanta-based "anchor organization" Project South and a veteran of the US civil rights movement, pointed out: "The [grassroots democratic] process, which we built, did not come naturally. The moment in which you start organizing, that moment you develop the culture of a group, and that culture is so difficult to change."[14] Atlanta-based founders' intersectional translating practices aimed at avoiding the establishment of a dominant group culture from the very first meeting, to make sure questions of leadership and problematic coalition dynamics could be discussed openly and inclusively (Blee 2012).

In Atlanta, misunderstandings between grassroots activists and professional staffers from institutional organizations included racism as a key issue. With the aim of avoiding conflicts between these groups at future events, the USSF team set up "intentional" workshops on the policy issues that both sides cared about,

---

[13] My interview, Detroit, May 25, 2010.
[14] My fieldnotes, National Planning Assembly, May 25, 2010, Detroit.

carefully planning the meeting choreography and the choice of speakers and facilitators following the principles of political translation. These policy-oriented workshops provided an open space for mutual learning and intercultural education, connecting the NGOs and funders with a variety of local grassroots groups.

NGO spokespersons and institutional funders who walked into the first of these workshops on immigration reform during the USSF event in Detroit showed little optimism; one institutional policy expert from a Washington, DC, NGO declared herself "skeptical."[15] The workshop began with a large plenary assembly opened and chaired by grassroots immigrant organizers, most of them students – the "radical locals," whom the policy experts had described as "dogmatic" and whose ideologies they had openly rejected in national coalition meetings.

Observing the interactions during the immigration workshop, I was surprised to see a reversal of typical relationships between professional and grassroots activists. Professional activists listened attentively to immigrant organizers. Workshop organizers asked all of the participants to join small groups, each composed of some members of NGOs and funders, as well as immigrant workers, student and youth activists, and local organizers. A USSF organizer explained how this heterogeneous group composition was a conscious political act: "We try to bring together different localized groups that are all very sectorial; we try to build convergence between them."[16] To avoid an asymmetric format in which the professional activists used the workshop to promote their own ideas without listening to the grassroots, political translators prepared the local leaders beforehand. As another USSF organizer from Project South explained, "To start dialogue, it's easy to get overwhelmed and fail to connect on the issue you are specifically interested in. In the Social Forum, we gave our members tasks, gave them business cards of the people whom they were to meet. We made them fundraise, so they could go there [to attend the meeting]. Each morning we met for a briefing."[17] This collective preparation for encountering professional activists proved success-ful for grassroots activists, whom I saw exchange business cards and self-consciously discuss proposals for cooperation.

By the end of the workshop, the professional activists whom I had interviewed right before the workshop had lost some of their skepticism, showing greater understanding toward local grassroots activists. The interactions had helped them connect emotionally to the grassroots. One said:

Okay, I am much less critical after the workshop than I was before. This is one of the unique spaces for us to talk to the other part. The growing sector in immigration mobilization is a sleeping giant, a potential force of power. People are very militant and

---

[15] My interview, USSSF 2010, Detroit, June 22, 2010.
[16] My interview with an organizer from Project South, Detroit, May 25, 2010.
[17] My interview with a USSF organizer, Detroit, May 17, 2010.

frustrated. To legalize these young people is the last thing the Republicans want because they would then have a young Left. Emotionally I give the US Social Forum an A; it makes you feel included. There is a big disconnection between DC and the Social Forum, but most of our work is to work for legislation as [a] movement. Atlanta and Detroit make you feel less alone. That's a powerful feeling, especially in the US; that's a big deal.[18]

Interviewees like this one moved from portraying immigrant youth as radical ideologues to seeing them as a new "young Left." Having fought second-generation–immigrants' radical proposals during the preparation phase, they now adopted a more self-reflective perspective. The workshops seem even to have helped participants from different ideological backgrounds to understand each other better.

After their initial encounters with the USSF, many local grassroots activists and community organizers had refrained from investing more time and money to participate in the national coalition meetings. Without the persuasion of the political translators, many grassroots leaders would probably not have attended national USSF coalition meetings – and they were not the only community that was reluctant to attend. According to Jody:

People in the US were very inexperienced. They are so much in their own communities. Also traditional community organizers. For them, it means opening up to the rest, they are so much [tied to] to their local community only, or to black organizing. [Outreach] was often face to face so that people trusted us. In the end, people said we don't know what the hell a Social Forum means, but we trust you and we'll come.[19]

Jody and her team members quickly began to realize that their processes of inclusion had to involve the political translation of class differences as well as differences in sexual orientation. Lesbians, gays, and transgender people were entering the Social Forum as newcomers. Following their experiences of homophobia in everyday life, the LGBT activists, among them many young people of color, were less inclined than others to attend USSF national coalition meetings and Social Forum events. The political translators thus made a plan:

We also made teaching sessions for people three weeks before Atlanta on our planned gender-neutral bathroom – so that the queer folk who don't identify with the Left can feel part of it, [so] that they come to the forum. For example, there were these Bible ladies, from the South, black, and we explained to them, we asked them, what it meant to have a women's-only bathroom. It was a reflection [*opening up to the idea of using a gender-neutral bathroom*] that started also for them. Why is it important? For queers, this difference [*of having a gender-neutral bathroom as an additional option*] made a huge contribution. It changed so much.[20]

Political translation thus came to include introducing newcomers, such as black church community members from the rural South, to new and unfamiliar

[18] My interview, USSSF 2010, Detroit, June 22, 2010.
[19] My interview, New York City, March 18, 2011.
[20] My interview, New York City, March 18, 2011.

practices, such as having a gender-neutral bathroom. Jody and other USSF political translators used their own multifaceted identities and backgrounds to help mainstream women understand the other groups. However, the political translators did not try to act as educators. Rather than explicitly advocating for minorities in meetings, they worked at changing the cultural codes of address and the spatial design of meetings, as I will illustrate below, so that disadvantaged groups could have a voice themselves. In Jody's words: "It's a translation of space, of gender that occurs in meetings."[21]

A scene at the beginning of a USSF workshop on gender justice in 2010 in Detroit exemplifies this translation of space. The door to the workshop is closed. A young African American USSF organizer stands at the entrance with a pink sign, welcoming me and other white middle-class participants and academics. Smiling, she continues to hold the door closed. She tells me that inside the workshop we will encounter participants from different backgrounds, some of whom have never before spoken in public. She invites us to treat each other respectfully and listen to each other's different experiences. "Is that OK with you?" I nod, and the door opens.[22]

Along with the other white, middle-class participants, I enter the room feeling as if I have entered a magical tent. I get a leaflet informing me about the organizers and the aim of the meeting, which is to build transnational and intersectional connections on gender justice issues. The meeting is fairly mixed in terms of race/ethnicity and gender backgrounds. As the presenters introduce themselves, I note that white participants and academics are not the majority among the invited speakers.

"I am from Bahrain," says the first invited expert speaker in the inner circle.[23] Another presenter, who seems agitated and almost afraid to speak, starts to talk about their experience as a transgender person. In the European meetings I attended, I never heard a transgender person tell their personal story of struggle and political activism. Everyone listens attentively, and the room is silent enough to hear a needle fall. Another speaker, an immigrant to the United States from Nairobi, talks about her experiences connecting African activists with immigrant women and domestic workers in New York City. Having attended the national preparatory assembly for the USSF in Detroit, I am not surprised to see immigrant women, people of color, and LGBT activists leading the discussion, although these groups felt marginalized in the ESF and in the GSF, whereas here they clearly feel much more at home. Following the workshop, one of the white participants who sat next to me is significantly impressed:

"I always thought of myself as simply a normal woman. But this workshop made me come to think about how I'm actually white and heterosexual."[24]

---

[21] My interview, New York City, March 18, 2011.   [22] My fieldnotes.   [23] My fieldnotes.
[24] My fieldnotes.

On the other hand, some of the highly educated and privileged long-term activists experienced emotional costs adapting to this situation:

I've been part of global justice groups for many years, but I had never before in my life worked in an organization with people of color. If you were a white person who wanted to be part of the [USSF] organizing committee, you must pass through an antiracist education. Otherwise they wouldn't accept you. I have never experienced this before. After the Social Forum experience, I think I'm able to continue to work together. Now I have made friends with others, [race] no longer matters. But it was weird.[25]

A few white, male, heterosexual-identified coalition members who held leadership positions inside the USSF complained about being forced to participate in workshops on gender equality or racial justice; they already saw themselves as feminist and antiracist. Yet even they ended by describing the workshops on antiracism and gender justice as efficient spaces for facilitating cooperation in the planning assembly. This interviewee's perspective also reflects the issue of clashing *habits* of interaction among different networks of global justice activists (Flesher 2015). As in the ESF (Chapter 1), several American professional activists in dominant national leadership positions of resource-rich organizations reported how the critical interventions by political translators changed their style of interacting with other groups, in particular, with immigrants and ethnic minorities or people of color (Chapter 1).

Participants with varying educational backgrounds also had trouble making mutual connections (Leondar-Wright 2014). For example, during a USSF plenary meeting in Detroit that I attended, a number of digital-media activists, many of them white graduate students, enthusiastically announced to the assembly that their group invited newcomers to join their media team to set up Internet communication technologies for the 2010 USSF: "We want everyone to join us!"[26] Yet, some had difficulties interacting with local grassroots media activists who in many cases had not profited from access to postgraduate education. For example, during a coffee break that had just been announced in order to foster collaboration, a local grassroots social-media activist, herself a second-generation immigrant, approached a member from the national media team, saying, "Hi, my name is Maria. How can we work together?" The two talked for a couple of minutes, then the national media coordinator departed without exchanging contact information. The immigrant, who worked locally with social-media groups, seemed disappointed: "Too bad," she commented to me. "I would have loved to talk more." Access to the USSF's national ICT team would have remained limited to a few participants, most from highly educated and privileged backgrounds, if political translators had not intervened.

In encounters like this one, political translators who formed part of the USSF team intervened informally to avoid or undo positional misunderstandings.

---

[25] My interview, USSF Detroit, June 23, 2010.   [26] My fieldnotes.

They were aware of differing group-specific cultures of online and offline communication (Mattoni 2012). Within the digital-media activist group, graduate students were accustomed to cooperating in loose, individualized networks, communicating across geographic distance and within transnational networks (Juris 2008a; Mattoni 2012; Pleyers 2010). They emphasized a problem-solving, efficiency-oriented work ethic – "getting things done." They chatted online rather than face to face. In contrast, older immigrants who worked locally with undocumented youth and community members stressed the importance of social encounters, emotional connections, and the creation of face-to-face social community. These differences between relatively individualized and more community-oriented ways of interacting also reflect class-related cultural differences (Lichterman 1996; Leondar-Wright 2014). Without political translators' presence as a third, cooperation would have been difficult between these subgroups.

Miguel Azahar was a social-media activist and a language justice translator. In many of the planning assembly sessions, he seemed to be observing rather than speaking, silently sitting behind his computer at the back of meetings. Following heated conflict within plenary discussions or during communication breakdowns, he would chat during coffee breaks with those he thought had felt marginalized or wanted to be better connected to others: "To build a national USSF, with these demographics, this work is simply a necessity," he said.[27] He rarely intervened in public assemblies, although he had long experience in bilingual, local groups involving citizens and immigrants. His working expertise in political translation in fact came from his work with environmentalist groups cooperating with grassroots union organizers. In translating from Spanish to English, he had first been a linguistic interpreter, then slowly learned how to hold a third position between the English-speaking majority members and Spanish-speaking immigrant workers: "For me," he said, "it started with my local group. I had never done this [work] before, but I found out I was good at translating. And I have done it since then."[28]

The USSF team thus produced not one homogeneous political translating practice but rather many different styles of cultural, linguistic, and intersectional translating. While some USSF organizers became experienced in taking the position of the translating third through their work within multilingual American social movement groups, others used practices inspired by women of color and community organizations. Still others, such as Jody, drew heavily on the experience of LGBT activists. Yet despite these variations, I observed a shared political translating style that united individuals from different backgrounds. For example, in all USSF meetings that I attended, Jody and other radical USSF founders who informally took turns as political translators during controversial plenary discussions refrained from acting as consensus facilitators. Instead, local grassroots activists from different

[27] My interview, Detroit, May 25, 2010.   [28] My interview, May 25, 2010, Detroit.

backgrounds served as facilitators in the deliberations. Miguel explained why USSF team members who specialized in intervening during cultural misunderstandings let local activists take the primary role of facilitators, themselves remaining in the background: "We are not here to facilitate decisions. What translators do is to give access to dialogue and information."[29]

Miguel, Jody, Will, and other USSF team members never interrupted immigrants or local grassroots members. If Jody or another political translator intervened, it was always in situations of positional misunderstandings in which a facilitator or dominant group member risked marginalizing another member.

Several other proactive, structural political translation practices during USSF plenary discussions amplified the voices in the coalition. First, USSF team members made each of their national planning assemblies accessible to undocumented immigrants by facilitating transportation and accommodations and by granting funding opportunities. Second, they located the first national USSF event in a place where immigrants'-rights organizations and other grassroots groups could attend with relative ease. Jody explained the USSF's efforts to make their events more accessible:

For example, since September 11 it is very difficult for undocumented immigrants to travel by plane, so we made other options available, and made sure they knew their rights. We also took care of this during the Social Forum event in Atlanta. Luckily we had no deportations.[30]

Indeed, local grassroots community organizers among USSF leaders I interviewed felt that their voices had an impact within the deliberation in the USSF national planning assembly, not only in influencing decisions but also in improving the atmosphere in meetings. For example, according to a second-generation immigrant who worked with undocumented immigrants in California, "Here in the USSF, translation has two effects. First, people's voices get heard. Second, I have seen the physical transformation in the room where people who are usually at the margin. They tell their stories for the first time and people hear their stories!"[31] Another grassroots organizer commented on how political translators' interventions before meetings and their presence during discussions avoided domination by a handful of speakers: "I have been organizing women of color and people of low income for thirty years. This here is not at all an 'American-style' meeting. In a good meeting like this one, people feel heard but speak as little as possible."[32]

Although the immigrants and grassroots community leaders in Atlanta felt empowered by the practices of political translation and their impact on decision-making, some of the funders and institutional supporters of the USSF were not pleased. They saw themselves losing power when the USSF founders

---

[29] My interview, May 25, 2010, Detroit.   [30] My interview, New York City, March 18, 2011.
[31] My interview, Detroit, June 24, USSF.
[32] My interview with an organizer, USSF 2010, Detroit, June 24, 2010.

decided to include a large number of minority leaders, among of them many grassroots activists, in their national planning assembly. This meant that institutional funders were faced with a new and more heterogeneous national coalition setting in which they no longer represented the majority of voices present. Jody explained,

We as a collective were really conscious of who was invited to be part of the National Planning Committee: the oppressed – 70 percent people of color and First Nations people, over 50 percent women and women-identified people, over 30 percent under thirty years old and a large visibility of LGBT, overwhelmingly people from the South and from the [local] region [*around Atlanta*]. We said we needed a great political team for the national planning assembly and we don't just want translation to be something where translators just sum up what [immigrants] tell. For [the US Social Forum in] Atlanta, we consulted forty grassroots organizations and thirty more professional white-collar organizations.[33]

In the end, with forty seats reserved for grassroots leaders and only thirty for "white-collar organizations," the institutional professional organizers working for large NGOs in Washington, DC, were no longer a majority on the USSF organizing team. As one of Jody's cotranslators commented,

In the US, the grassroots sector, the working class, poor, people of color, women, and LGBTQ [people] took leadership of the USSF process and set the table, set the agenda. We did not see that in WSF leadership or in the forces put forward in US social justice spaces. We determined that our process was to be "open" – no one turned away – but we were intentional about the leadership of the process, the demands put forward, the voices heard and who sat on the National Planning Committee.[34]

In their work of political translation, USSF founders consciously broke with the ideas of decentralized or direct democracy based on the model of neutral facilitation. Jody, Miguel, Will, and other USSF leaders were neither representative leaders nor facilitators, but kept themselves in the powerful though highly informal third position as political translators, holding together the fragile coalition. Nevertheless, Jody and the other self-affirmed political translators probably exerted more influence on the proceedings than any other group. Might this emergent model create invisible domination? A decision about funding provides an avenue for exploring this question.

FUNDING: FRANKFURT AND ATLANTA COMPARED

Following the initial meeting in Frankfurt, the GSF experienced a funding crisis. In early 2004 unions affiliated with the Social Democrat government in office had little interest in supporting the GSF, which opposed their government's workfare reforms (Andretta and Reiter 2009). This funding gap soon created a stalemate in

---

[33] My interview, New York City, March 18, 2010.
[34] E-mail interview with a USSF founder, May 15, 2011.

the national preparatory meetings, as the Left Party promised funding, but did not respect the proposals of the much larger group of "locals," the grassroots activists who were organizing the national preparatory assembly.

The conflict over funding escalated during a GSF national preparatory meeting in May of 2004, as the facilitators of the meeting unilaterally supported the Left Party–funders' proposal to organize a national Social Forum event in the ethnically homogeneous eastern German town of Erfurt, in a region known for its latent far-right-wing radicalism. A grassroots activist described this conflict:

Why did they choose Erfurt? It was clear that in this location, there could not be much mobilization. I am active in several local groups and local social forums, and I do not understand. They did not trust us.[35]

This distrust of locals seemed to be rooted in a deep lack of mutual understanding. In interviews with GSF facilitators and professional activists from the German Left Party, I found that the town of Erfurt fit the funders' party interests. Because the German Left Party had its grassroots base in eastern Germany, members of that party saw Erfurt as a venue from which to reach out to that base. A professional activist from the German Left Party who facilitated GSF meetings with Harald said:

For [the first German] Social Forum [event to take place in the city of] Erfurt, we wanted to convince forty millions of Germans of the possibility of another world. The locals on the national preparatory assembly have made this difficult for us.[36]

Selecting Erfurt, rather than a larger city – such as Berlin, Frankfurt, Hamburg, Munich, or even Stuttgart – meant going against the strong preference of the grassroots activists, who were concerned that Erfurt might be unsuitable for immigrants and minorities. But the facilitators and professional activists justified their choice of Erfurt on pragmatic grounds. One said:

Conditions for organizing a Social Forum in Germany were difficult, and then when [Wolfgang] got the Erfurt mayor into our boat without necessarily asking all other groups in the assembly, this was immediately interpreted as factionalism.[37]

As soon as Harald and his team of facilitators, which included Wolfgang and Peter, obtained funding from the mayor of Erfurt, in May of 2004, they went public in a German newspaper to announce their decision to hold the assembly there. However, they did not communicate with grassroots activists who also formed part of the German national preparatory assembly and who learned about this unilateral decision from news coverage. These groups felt betrayed.

---

[35] Interview with a local GSF organizer from the Bremen Social Forum, Erfurt, July 21, 2005; conducted in German, my translation into English.

[36] Interview with Harald during the Istanbul preparatory assembly to the ESF, September 9, 2005; conducted in German, my translation into English.

[37] Interview with a GSF facilitator, Istanbul, September 9, 2005; conducted in German, my translation into English.

In an "open letter," a grassroots activist from a local Social Forum group spoke for many other participants who were part of the national Social Forum preparatory group:

Dear Wolfgang,
   You three, Harald, Peter, and you have at least organized one [informal] meeting [with the funder and Left Party mayor of] Erfurt in April 2004 ... Self-mandated, you have given the impression to [funders and activists in] Erfurt that you were legitimized by the [national preparatory assembly] of the Social Forum process in Germany. Through this you have positioned yourself in a leadership position, abusing an author-ity that had been built collectively by all participants in the national preparatory assembly beforehand ... You have been making the assembly decide a Social Forum that you had already decided ...[38]

After this letter was sent, 60 percent of the participants who formed part of the German national preparatory assembly and 80 percent of the local grassroots activists collectively quit the national Social Forum process.[39] When immigrants and local groups chose to exit, after several years of loyal commitment, the large and culturally diverse grassroots base of the global justice movement in Germany split off from the GSF coalition.

   In the course of this crisis, grassroots members of leftist unions and parties involved in the GSF planning group admitted that these leaders had made mistakes. In the words of one: "At the national level, friendship could not emerge because domination from some of us has suffocated democracy."[40] The facilitators, however, were unaware of these positional misunderstandings with their grassroots base. In the last interview I conducted with Harald, he said, "I still do not understand why we did not become friends with each other on the national preparatory assembly. If only I knew."[41]

   How did the USSF leaders avoid this kind of breakdown? Instead of complying with their funders' proposals concerning the content and timing of their planned national Social Forum event, the USSF founders deliberately chose to build trust with local grassroots groups and assumed a third, translating position in negotiations with funders.

   A first key strategic decision that the Atlanta team of leaders and translators in the United States handled differently than the GSF team was to decline an early funding offer in 2003 that entailed hosting a national USSF grassroots democratic forum within a short period of time. "We were risking a lot," USSF leader-translator Jody explained, regarding this moment of uncertainty.[42] While funders wanted the USSF event to happen as soon as possible, the Social Forum's founders

---

[38] http://listi.jpberlin.de/pipermail/offenerraum/2005-January/000020.html, accessed January 7, 2005.
[39] My fieldnotes based on participant observation.
[40] My interview, Berlin, January 30, 2010; conducted in German, my translation into English.
[41] My interview, Berlin, January 30, 2010; conducted in German, my translation into English.
[42] My interview, New York City, March 18, 2010.

opted to invest more time for extending their national leadership to include members of traditionally disadvantaged groups.

In contrast to the GSF coalition leaders, the USSF grassroots organizers could not hope to rely on established political parties and unions to fund them but depended instead on meager support from progressive philanthropic funders (Guerrero 2010). In past decades, elite foundations have notably improved their outreach to resource-poor social movement initiatives in the United States. However, they have also imposed their own professionalized organizing models (Guerrero 2008, 2010; Minkoff and Agnone 2010). In the case of the USSF, the funders had announced that they wanted to support a national Social Forum event in the United States. However, they declined to support what they perceived as an "unprofessional" national USSF planning committee. Because Jody and her team had created a national planning team that included a large majority of "non-professionals" – people of color and women leaders representing local grassroots groups – funders backed away.

As in Germany, the problem was the professionals' distrust of local grassroots groups. The funders offered to support the USSF only on condition that it be organized by well-established organizations whose spokespersons they knew.

USSF founder Will remembered negotiations with funders: "They said: who is in? Why don't you include those NGOs, and why not those? We don't trust you to do it."[43] The local grassroots organizers in the USSF planning committee were outraged, assuming that the funders wanted their own donor constituency to be better reflected among organizations. One said, "Officially, they'd say: which groups do you include? They framed it officially in terms of capacity. It was white supremacy."[44] The funders in turn were important. According to a funder interested in the USSF who worked for a small progressive foundation supporting people of color:

Practically, it's not about power-sharing. [Money] makes participatory democracy impossible, or very difficult. Because there is a scarcity of financial resources, there is huge competition, and there are huge differences among funders.[45]

The funders felt that they had to adhere to a restricted schema for selecting fund-worthy organizations based on competitive, policy-oriented criteria. These criteria generally made it easier for national-level NGOs with professionalized staff to apply. Organizational scholars have analyzed the dilemma of liberal elite foundations and the US sector of social movement philanthropy in the context of market-based competition and scarce resources (Minkoff and Agnone 2010). This interaction seems a prime example. As a result, potential funders obliged USSF organizers to include a much larger number of

---

[43] My interview, Detroit, May 25, 2010.   [44] Informal communication.
[45] My interview, Detroit, June 26, 2010.

professionalized, well-funded NGOs and "white-collar organizations" in their leadership team.

When the USSF team turned down funding in order to accommodate their vision of inclusiveness, the lack of funding caused a second internal conflict. They now lacked the money to pay for linguistic interpretation equipment. Finally, the resource-poor immigrant organizations themselves provided the equipment. Will, who was among the local hosts of the first USSF in his home town of Atlanta, recalled these tensions: "We did not get in funders, and so we again and again debated this question [of how to get funding]."[46]

The tensions around funding led to a split within the original group of USSF founders. Some USSF team members, including Miguel, who worked on the issue of including linguistic minorities and immigrants, ended by foregoing any payment for their services. As Miguel told me:

It was a battle to get language access for Atlanta. It was a battle to get [at least one linguistic interpreter-translator] employed for one month that last time. [The national planning assembly of the US Social Forum] didn't want to spend money; in the end, we had to work as volunteers.[47]

Because of their explicit position on the side of the immigrant groups, the political translators were not speaking as a pure third voice in these deliberations. The split created tensions and – despite a strong desire to understand – positional misunderstanding on both sides.

On the other hand, the solidarity and strong commitment of some of the political translators in the contentious debates about USSF funding changed the atmosphere and stimulated a new visibility for immigrants and other minorities. Given a venue for public expression, minority groups realized that they could significantly influence decision-making if they worked together. For example, in a charged discussion in the national planning assembly that I observed, activists who worked with people with disabilities came in to address the immigrants' linguistic and political needs.

There are a lot of people in the assembly who make a living [out of their work as professional activists] and who give a shit whether their organization spends money on language access. They have no awareness. They say, "Now I need that translation – now, now, now." People who provide language access are treated like plumbers. The access question is sensitive for people with disabilities as well . . . I can understand the fear of the National Planning Assembly to make a commitment and then not have the resources . . . And still I tell you it makes a big impact that [you] are here and that you speak.[48]

The essential trade-off entailed in political translation became clear during these contentious debates about funding. As a result of their own ethos of power-sharing, the professional activists among the founders of the USSF who had

---

[46] My interview, Detroit, June 26, 2010.   [47] My Interview, Detroit, May 25, 2010.
[48] My interview, Detroit, May 25, 2010.

initiated political translation themselves lost a good part of their influence to the minority activists and grassroots activists they wanted to empower. Jody put it:

My partner always says they don't call it "the struggle" for nothing. I did not always win in conversations. But the process is to create something together with people whom you don't even like, with whom you would not like to be friends.[49]

Political translators like Jody were willing to pay the cost of accepting cooperation with group members whose identity and ideologies they "disliked," forming relationships that transcended and transformed boundaries of taste, culture, ideology, and class. This ethos of accepting the costs sheds light on why the political translators did not become established as dominant leaders, as one might have expected given their prominent role in the center of organizing the coalition. Although Jody and her co-organizers did not submit to the demands of the institutional supporters and funders, to a certain degree they did "surrender" to "radical locals" on the National Planning Assembly who took decisions that went against the initial plans formulated by Jody and her cofounders – for example, regarding the location of meetings and the schedule of planned USSF events. Surrender depicts, among other things, the quality of accepting the loss of *a part* of one's identity as a sovereign leader (Wagner-Pacifici 2005). Giving up one's leadership position *by sharing it with someone else* requires an acknowledgment of fragility, interconnectedness, and interdependence with others (Wagner-Pacifici 2005). As political translators, Jody and her cofounders experienced this necessary compromise ambivalently as both painful and positive, a process that deepened the relationship of equality and cooperation that they had fought for.

The conflicts with funders and the painful processes within their coalition eventually paid off. Grassroots activists who saw their voices more equally recognized in decision-making about finances contributed most of the preparatory work in logistics and hosting the first USSF event in Atlanta, mainly through unpaid voluntary work by their local community organizations. The process created an even greater sharing of power among previously disparate groups. But new conflicts arose because different groups had contributed and "owned" unequal resources. The local grassroots leaders who had agreed to host the first-ever USSF event in Atlanta had to intervene as political translators to build trust between groups whose members did not necessarily "like" or know each other's styles. As one of the Atlanta founders told me:

There were really challenging moments. For example, the prepayment of the hotel rooms. Who would sign those contracts? There were forty to seventy organizations in the planning committee. I said, we have to sign them together. That was a political struggle. You have to build trust once you realize what kind of infrastructure you need to

[49] My interview, New York City, March 18, 2010.

build a political process! I think that we have learnt a very important lesson – it made us rely on grassroots fundraisers; we had to pass the hat at each meeting![50]

Several years passed before organizers were able to save enough money through their own grassroots-based fundraising to finance the planned grassroots democratic forum. Yet the practice by which USSF coalition founders worked at "building trust" among the heterogeneous coalition members they had brought together was, by and large, successful. The coalition now included job centers as well as student organizations, labor, immigrant organizations, North American indigenous people and black and Latino church-based organizations, many of them headed by women and female or queer-identified leaders. This strategy entailed both extremely hard work and financial vulnerability for the political translators and their organizations. Jody told me: "We got a bit of funding really very late, very shortly before the Atlanta Social Forum."[51] That last-minute funding came mostly from structurally underfunded local grassroots organizations in the Southern civil rights movement, traditional church organizations, and their supporters (Guerrero 2008).

Although most traditional funders and institutional supporters had given up on the USSF, Jody, Will, and the seventy co-organizers on the national planning assembly of the USSF were surprised by their success both in finding funding at the grassroots and in generating participation. After years of intense negotiations with local leaders and institutional supporters, the first national Social Forum event in Atlanta brought together many more people than the organizers had hoped for. Ten thousand participants attended the first USSF in Atlanta, and almost twenty thousand participants traveled to a similar event in Detroit (Karides et al. 2010; Smith et al. 2010).

Given the meager resources of the USSF coalition, as well as the lack of institutional funding and support (Fantasia 2010), neither international nor American observers predicted this success. In contrast to the declining participation in the GSF and other national Social Forums in Europe in the aftermath of the global economic crisis, the USSF launched three policy-oriented campaigns on immigration reform, climate change, and vulnerable workers (Karides et al. 2010). Regarding precarious or vulnerable labor, the USSF encouraged the foundation of two major national coalitions, the National Alliance of Domestic Workers and the cross-sectorial Excluded Workers Congress (Poo et al. 2010). Each of these grassroots coalitions united vulnerable workers and global justice activists across many intersections, including immigrants and groups from different linguistic, ethnic, national, and social backgrounds (Poo et al. 2010; Smith et al. 2010). USSF founders co-initiated a nationwide decentralized urban protest network on the "Right to the City" – one of the germ cells of the Occupy Wall Street movement, whose

[50] My interview, New York City, March 19, 2010.
[51] My interview, New York City, March 19, 2010.

protests against inequality occurred in 2011, one year after the USSF summit in Detroit (Mayer 2009a; Smith 2017; Gitlin 2012; Juris 2012; Schneider 2013).

Despite the challenges of funding scarcity and financial inequality, the most relevant outcome of the USSF was probably that political translation facilitated an extremely heterogeneous national coleadership model, involving both minority groups and resource-poor local activist groups who had never before engaged in coalition with one another. Local grassroots activists who had felt most skeptical about the challenging internal conflicts around race now saw the USSF as a strategic and political success. One said:

The [USSF groups] have made the greatest advantage in the past two to three years in the US Left. They created a space where labor can interact with people of color and where the peace movement can interact with the grassroots. And they made a huge radical contribution. They provided a meeting space where transgender and intersexual people are part of the actual organization and where these and other people can meet them. And by this they were years ahead of local coalitions in this country that I've been organizing myself.[52]

More surprising than the positive feedback given by local grassroots activists was the evolution among institutional supporters who had initially kept their distance from the USSF. The Ford Foundation and other progressive donors now promised future funding, according to USSF founder Will:

In the first USSF in Atlanta, the meeting with funders was suddenly packed with sixty people, all enthusiasts, suddenly. "This is incredible!" they said. They asked how we managed to bring all these people. It was a miracle that this happened. "How was this possible?" they asked. "And so new! How did you get ten thousand participants from nothing?" And yet, to look back at how this happened, particularly in the US: it was not natural. The lesson to me: you build a much better foundation if you're forced to rely on your own and if you resist [attempts at cooptation].[53]

In a broader, long-term perspective, for many professional activists, the cross-sectorial coalition workshops on immigration and other themes organized by the USSF team turned out to be transformative experiences that changed their thinking about democracy and strategy in the US Left. Reflecting on her first encounter with grassroots activists in the context of the USSF several years after the Atlanta Social Forum, one pragmatist said:

At the time, I devalued any intersectional cross-coalition building process in which people of color take a leadership position and which is really relationship building. I still hate the "process," but now I have these relationships and they are really important for my work. My critiques at the time were very utilitarian. Now I have good relationships with people whom I at the time criticized and with whom I work together all the time.[54]

---

[52] My interview, Detroit, June 25, 2010.   [53] My interview, New York City, March 19, 2010.
[54] My interview, South Hadley, November 20, 2015.

However, deeper ideological battles in the American Left continued to create conflicts between the professional pragmatists and the radical leaders supporting the USSF and its work. From the perspective of NGOs and institutional organizations, the political translation by the USSF team, which brought minorities into leadership positions at Atlanta, came with a strategic cost of losing majority-white Americans and mainstream supporters of the Democratic Party. One such mainstream supporter acknowledged that "the USSF left me with more tools." However, she continued, "It is cut off; it's a particular window on these issues. For example, [on] the Middle East, it's very sectarian, very pro-Palestine; one side is simply excluded." She believed that "the existing space [must] be extended for different factions of the Left to come together."[55]

When I confronted USSF leader-translators with these critiques, they agreed, at least in part. USSF founder Jody said she was fully aware that her coalition was still missing a large spectrum of moderate Left institutional supporters close to the Democratic Party. Political translators had won the ideological battle over funding by deciding not to take funds that would have forced them to abandon their grassroots democratic model. Yet, another part of the political translation process involves learning to lose ideological battles. For example, Jody saw that her model of political translation had inadvertently limited her and other professional activists' influence on strategic decisions made by the Atlanta national planning assembly:

It is true. There is no clear roadmap how to make things better. I did not always get what I wanted. For example, the question about having a plenary about the Middle East. But the longer you build that relationship, the more it's about what you create together. That's to me the beauty of the Social Forum: it's that you get to know what's possible.

Anthropologists have shown how the process of cultural and linguistic translating can transform professionals into witnesses of the inequality suffered by those for whom they translate, creating an empathetic understanding of the others' position (Sanford 2003). This was the case for professional activists among the USSF organizers. Jody described the humility she had learned: "Just because I'm a woman and queer, that does not mean I'm always right. People of color are not right just because they are people of color. The process is learning that. We're also in a process of individual and collective transformation."[56]

Jody's reflections on the Atlanta coalition point to a broader open question for the US Left today: how to create a broad and diverse Left coalition that is able to fight the radical right (Juris 2013; McAdam and Kloos 2014; Meyer and Pullum 2015). For example, in Atlanta, USSF founders practiced what Jody called "intentional" outreach to include minorities and traditionally disadvantaged populations. Jeff Juris has critically examined the concept of "intentional" organizing used by the Atlanta coalition to explore how it excluded white middle-class activists and other sectors of the US Left, including large policy-

---

[55] My interview, Detroit, June 24, 2010.   [56] My interview, New York City, March 18, 2010.

oriented NGOs, more bureaucratic organizations, such as trade unions, and anarchists and direct-action activists (Juris 2008, 2013). In Chapter 4, I will discuss the example of a collective of local political translators who self-consciously decided to perform "intentional" outreach to both *mainstream* actors of institutional politics and *minorities* in order to build fair and inclusive participatory democracy in a Californian city struggling with rising poverty, rising rents, and gentrification.

Political translation provided the founding model for the USSF coalition, and yet it remained an ephemeral practice. Carried out by a loose network of mainly grassroots global justice organizers, it lasted as long as these individuals were present. After having built the USSF coalition and organized two major USSF events in Atlanta in 2007 and in Detroit in 2010, Jody and other political translators moved on to support emerging grassroots coalitions on climate justice, on the Right to the City, and on the organizing of coalitions among different groups of excluded workers (Goldberg et al. 2012; Smith 2017; see also Mayer 2009a).

DISCUSSION: POLITICAL TRANSLATION AND DIVERSE LEADERSHIP IN THE US LEFT

In the USSF coalition, political translation was as much about the translation of marginalized knowledge as it was about power. It catapulted a new generation of immigrants, people of color, LGBT activists, and minority organizers to the center of national leadership within the US radical global justice movement. Both established staffers from NGOs and local grassroots activists felt transformed by the experience of the USSF – admitting their initial challenges in connecting with people with whom they had little everyday experience, and eventually benefiting from the experience.

Political translation can serve as a democratic practice of leadership in the US progressive Left distinct from the model of rational neutral facilitation or instrumental strategic brokerage. Scholars have emphasized the strategic relevance of *brokers* within heterogeneous coalitions – that is, network leaders or intermediaries mediating between institutional and local groups such as those involved in national Social Forum coalitions (della Porta and Mosca 2007; Tarrow 2006). Some authors explore the cultural skills of "bridge leadership" required of grassroots leaders as intermediaries building bridges within heterogeneous coalitions (Robnett 1997; Roth 2003; Smith 2005; Wood 2005). However, the critical intentionality and disruptive character of processes of political translating and their potential transformative power haven't been acknowledged. Unlike previous bridge leaders, the USSF political translators' struggle was about not just local grassroots mobilization but national leadership. The political translating practices I have uncovered here are an emergent phenomenon directly influenced by the extraordinarily diverse, multilingual culture of global justice activism in the United States today.

What distinguished the political translation collective among USSF founders from previous bridge leaders and brokers was their culturally and linguistically diverse backgrounds – something that was important to an understanding of why these US-based activists would come to see their work as a translation of democracy, and not in an instrumental, strategic brokerage job. Their bilingual or multilingual skills were based on their professional experiences as organizers of local multiracial and multilingual grassroots organizations and churches, and as members of marginalized communities. In Atlanta, diversity was a condition for both the emergence and the outcome of the political translation process. Coming from different identity backgrounds and movements, USSF founders were able to bridge relatively successfully the differences of identity and structural inequality dividing the members in their national planning assembly.

The conscious and collective practices of activists like Jody who installed themselves as political translators in the USSF open a new perspective on the critical intentionality and the oppositional consciousness of marginalized groups within broader social movement coalitions (Ghaziani 2008; Juris et al. 2014; Leonard-Wright 2012). Political translators in Atlanta addressed the microdynamics of intersectional marginalization in the context of face-to-face interactions within coalitions, especially those that include resource-poor social movement organizations as well as professional NGOs and market-based philanthropic foundations (Smith 2005; Lépinard 2014; see also Whittier 2014). USSF founders' intersectional translating practices aimed at avoiding the establishment of a dominant group culture from the very first meeting, to make sure questions of leadership and problematic coalition dynamics could be discussed openly and inclusively (Blee 2012). Their success lay in holding a third position between the national institutional NGO sector and radical local grassroots activists and identity leaders, without silencing or submitting to pressures from institutional funders. They resisted pressure from white-collar organizations and funders to bring in their preferred speakers and impose their perspectives on the national planning assembly. Contemporary mobilizations in many parts of the world increasingly face this issue as they strive to encompass more diverse coalitions.

3

Santa Brigida, California

How Political Translation Failed at City Hall

In a political climate rife with debates concerning immigration and cultural diversity, many American and European cities have introduced participatory forums for democracy to build dialogue between established residents and resident immigrants and linguistic minorities (Alcalde 2016; Fung 2004; Nanz 2009). It makes a difference, however, who facilitates and *politically translates* participatory democracy in order to make it work in the adversarial context of local decision-making at city halls, where different groups compete for political offices and institutional power (Baiocchi 2005; Talpin 2006; Sintomer et al. 2016; McQuarrie 2015).

The experience of Santa Brigida,[1] California, illustrates how a group of political translators can become trapped in the logic of institutional power, seeming to embrace the very politics and ideas of institutional and economic power elites they had previously combated. It suggests that because power may corrupt political translation, people in positions of power can rarely be effective as intermediaries or representatives of disadvantaged communities.

In Santa Brigida, where Latino/as made up the majority of the city council, a number of bilingual, progressive city council members wanted to build dialogue between the English-speaking city officials and the socially disadvantaged groups in the town, especially linguistic minorities and Latino/a resident immigrants. For this purpose they set up a series of participatory citizen forums at the local city hall. I attended the last of these meetings in June 2010, documenting the deliberations that culminated in a final decision-making process.[2]

As the meeting commenced, city hall was filled with about two hundred participants eager to debate an urban redevelopment project that promised to provide affordable housing in an impoverished neighborhood consisting mainly of resident immigrants from Mexico and Central America. A threat was hanging over the meeting: the city's plan as written entailed the destruction of

---

[1] All names of locations, individuals, and groups in this chapter have been changed.

[2] My fieldnotes, Santa Brigida City Hall meeting, June 7, 2010.

residents' current homes without – residents believed – offering a sufficient number of alternative, affordable rental units. Rumor had it that city officials in fact intended to replace previously guaranteed affordable housing units with for-profit developments. Cognizant of the crowd's apprehension, the mayor – acting as meeting facilitator – grandly announced in his opening speech: "I promise that everyone will be heard tonight."

Yet several hours later, as the meeting wore on, many local participants began to express anger: clearly they did *not* feel heard, despite the provision of Spanish translation. One exasperated resident, Maria Silva, addressed the mayor directly in Spanish: "If you really wanted to listen to our demands about the urban-planning project, you could sit down at a round table and talk to us … You don't represent us." The bilingual mayor, responding in English, seemed impervious to her concerns: "Maria, I ask you to calm down. General comments are not allowed until the end of this session." The council members and city officials nodded.[3]

The "open" city hall meetings in Santa Brigida had been created following protest by community organizers who advocated broader access and participation, especially for the large population of low-income resident immigrants who did not speak English.

Following the mayor's response, Daniel Bueno, a progressive city councilman in his thirties, then spoke in English, both to Maria and to many of the other Spanish speakers in attendance:

If you say "I want to speak at city hall," you will get a chance to speak tonight. English is the dominant language of the US but a lot of materials by the city are now in Spanish, as the city council has become more representative. We decided to have a full-time professional interpreter, and there is headphone equipment, so also, even if you don't speak, you can listen.

Indeed, the council did provide bilingual interpretation at the meeting and also allowed community members to bring their own translators. And yet these provisions clearly did not assuage many residents' sense of disenfranchisement.

The problem in Santa Brigida was that at least some of the city council members were politically beholden to the commercial developers who contributed significantly to their campaigns and who backed the redevelopment plan. Others, however, like the city council member quoted, played an interesting "institutional political translator" role. Their idea was to build dialogue between English-speaking city officials and socially disadvantaged groups, including linguistic minorities and Latino/a resident immigrants.

The atmosphere at the last of the participatory city hall meetings on the planned redevelopment project was tense. At the beginning of the meeting, the white city staffers who acted as ushers politely asked formally dressed city council members, invited business representatives, developers, firefighters, and

[3] My fieldnotes, Santa Brigida City Hall meeting, June 7, 2010.

their families to sit in the front rows, where chairs had been reserved. As the assembly slowly filled and Latino/a working-class residents and their families started to take several rows of empty seats right behind public employees, the city staffers intervened. Speaking in English, they asked the residents, many of them women with small children, to leave the empty seats. An usher addressed a woman with a small child holding a balloon: "You are not allowed here with a balloon." Many of the residents had brought red balloons and T-shirts sporting the name of the community coalition, "SABAH," the Santa Brigida Alliance for Affordable Housing.

In this setting of overlapping linguistic barriers and disciplinary actions by city personnel, the community women took ushers' interventions as an exhortation to retreat to the back of the assembly. Although the council members had officially affirmed that families and children were at the center of debate about redevelopment, city council staff placed them in a visibly more marginal place than that of the financiers and public employees.

THE CONTEXT: DEMOGRAPHIC CHANGE, DIVERSITY, AND LOCAL DEMOCRACY IN SANTA BRIGIDA

One of the poorest cities in Southern California, Santa Brigida offers a particularly relevant case for assessing the empowering potential and limits of institutional political translation in the service of local participatory democracy in multilingual, culturally diverse communities. Many of the city's predominantly working-class residents hold service jobs in support of whiter, more affluent communities in the surrounding greater Los Angeles area. Every fifth Santa Brigida resident lives below the poverty line, taking in less than half the Californian median income.[4] In the past twenty years, the population of Santa Brigida has grown over 70 percent; the median age is currently twenty-nine years.[5] Over 70 percent of local households use Spanish as their first language, and almost 80 percent of residents identify as Hispanics, followed by 10 percent whites and 10 percent Asians.[6] Even excluding undocumented immigrants, resident immigrants and their children form a majority of the residents in Santa Brigida.

Following the demographic changes of the past decade, the city council's majority has shifted from predominantly white to predominantly Latino/a. The seven-member Santa Brigida City Council includes the mayor. The elected mayor, Tony Peña, has a history of promoting policies to address poverty and the dramatic shortage of affordable housing following rapid population growth. During his first term during the mid-eighties, he made it a priority to secure "Federal Empowerment Zone status for some of the City's most disadvantaged neighborhoods, delivering federal funds to build capital,

[4] US Census Bureau 2010.   [5] City of Santa Brigida documents.
[6] Facts about Santa Brigida. (City of Santa Brigida documents.)

increase employment and to provide needed services to these residents."[7] A business owner, Peña describes his role in relation to his employees as that of a "good father," a metaphor that he uses frequently for his chairing and facilitating role in the open city council meetings.[8]

Participatory democracy in Santa Brigida's open city hall meetings has for some years involved bimonthly open debates in which city council members hear citizens' and residents' demands on topics from the budget to urban planning and the policing of immigration. In these participatory-styled city hall meetings, three council members in particular saw themselves empowering monolingual Spanish residents and giving them a voice at city hall. Daniel Bueno, Sal Tijolero, and Samantha Clark had all promised in their campaigns for office to bring social and democratic change in order to facilitate the inclusion of Latino/as and immigrants. Just days before the high-stakes city hall meeting that I attended, Daniel Bueno had repeated this promise that the redevelopment project would include the creation of a new park for the neighborhood, as had been initially previewed: "We will make this possible for you, for us all: there will be a park!"[9] As Sal Tijolero put it: "We now have a majority at the city council, where people's voices really make a difference."[10]

This group's intent had been to affirm what I would call a *critical third position* between city government and the people. In Bueno's words, "We are bilingual; we understand people; we also get people's passion. Thanks to us in the city council, it is now a requirement that everything talked through in public has to be bilingual. In reality, the translator is for the audience because we council members understand people. We want people to understand we are their government, we want them to take part, be included, as half of the citizens in Santa Brigida were born outside the United States. We want to make sure they know that it is not just a few that make the decisions."[11] Samantha Clark put it this way: "I don't like to tell a personal story – but I slept on the floor as a kid. And as a policy-maker I want to change that. Here I sit with my colleagues and we can win battles."[12]

The three other city council members who were more allied with the mayor showed less enthusiasm for bilingual civic dialogue. They focused their work instead variously on finances, business, and the fight against crime. In contrast, Bueno held monthly office hours for community members to tell him their stories. Clark worked to increase the visibility of young Latina women, helping them to feel included in the business of the city and take an interest in participation by making them attend city council meetings and receive prizes

---

[7] City of Santa Brigida documents.
[8] My fieldnotes, Santa Brigida City Hall meeting, June 7, 2010.
[9] My fieldnotes, SABAH Community Forum, June 2, 2010.
[10] My fieldnotes, Santa Brigida City Hall meeting, June 7, 2010.
[11] My interview, Santa Brigida, June 20, 2010.
[12] My fieldnotes, SABAH Community Forum, June 2, 2010.

and decorations for their achievements in sports and culture. All three interacted bilingually in Spanish and English with residents in city council meetings.

The most contentious issue that arose during the open city hall meetings that I analyzed during a five-month period in 2010 was the proposed for-profit urban redevelopment project that was the focus of the final meeting. Amid crises of overpopulation, urban decline, and rising rents, the city planned to invest in a large-scale redevelopment project in the historic Marcy District. According to local news reports and official city documents, the City of Santa Brigida would offer a team of private, for-profit developers a loan to build a large-scale housing complex including "mixed low-income apartments with market-rate homes."[13] In return for the city loaning the development firm more than $18 million for the project, the developing companies pledged to keep almost all of the project's 112 apartments affordable for low- and very-low-income communities.[14] According to the official project proposal, the city council would make it a priority to provide affordable housing for low-income immigrant families now living in overcrowded units.[15]

Several city council members, including the mayor, owned property and had embedded financial interests connected to the redevelopment project. According to a report by the NGO SABRID, the Santa Brigida Responsible Development Cooperative, which is dedicated to affordable housing, the real estate and construction sectors are among the five top industries contributing approximately 60 percent of the monetary contributions to city council races and approximately 40 percent to mayoral campaigns.[16]

As part of opening up the redevelopment process to residents, the city set up a two-year participatory democratic "outreach" endeavor that included over twenty meetings with community members, the for-profit development firm, and city staffers without direct involvement of council members themselves.[17] In these meetings, the mayor and his allies on the council promoted the project as a major step toward revitalizing the historical neighborhood and bringing artists, bars, and shopping centers into a rundown area of historical buildings.[18] Residents and community and neighborhood organizations, however, feared that such gentrification would threaten poor families' access to housing and services, and began mobilizing a protest.[19]

---

[13] *Santa Brigida Gazette*, June 8, 2010. See also City of Santa Brigida Five-Year Implementation Plan, May 21, 2010.

[14] City of Santa Brigida documents. See also *Santa Brigida Gazette*, June 8, 2010.

[15] City of Santa Brigida documents. See also City of Santa Brigida Five-Year Implementation Plan, May 21, 2010.

[16] Research report on campaign contributions in Santa Brigida and neighboring communities, years 2004–2010, document provided by SABRID, page 10.

[17] City of Santa Brigida documents.

[18] *Santa Brigida Gazette*, June 8, 2010. *Santa Brigida News*, June 10.

[19] *Santa Brigida Gazette*, January 19, 2010, June 7, 2011.

The problem they saw was that, according to SABRID, the local NGO working on sustainable urban development, most low-income residents would be unable to pay the increased rents projected even for the new "affordable" housing units specified in the plan.[20]

I attended multilingual community gatherings, activist meetings, and city hall meetings from February to June 2010, in the last five months of the two-year period of the participatory process. Resistance to the project came from a large coalition of civic and community organizations that united as SABAH. Representatives of SABAH and another association, the Friends of the Historical Marcy Neighborhood, pointed out that two conservative city council members and the mayor owned property in the area affected by the planned redevelopment project.[21] This implied a direct conflict of interests, where city council members' financial interests had the potential to influence their political decision-making in favor of a decision suiting the investors' interests rather than the residents.

In May 2010, after participating in two years of project-related meetings organized by the city, community organizers saw their worst suspicions confirmed. A week before the last scheduled participatory city hall meeting, city hall officials announced their final proposal, which clearly favored private investors over affordable housing.[22] The number of affordable housing units had shrunk from more than one hundred, as was initially projected, to just seventy-six units, and within the segment of affordable units, most units now previewed a higher rent than previously agreed, with the monthly rent raised from less than $600 to $900 for two-bedroom apartments. This development meant that few of the current low-income residents would have been able to profit from the project as they earned too little money to even pay for the more affordable renting units. Once residents realized that city hall officials did not plan to include sufficient genuinely affordable housing and that they also had not considered any of the environmental sustainability concerns raised by residents in previous meetings, that final meeting became a high-stakes venue for residents to make last-ditch demands. The initial proposal had also included plans for a park, which, to the dismay of the members of the civic associations, was canceled as well. One member of the Friends of the Marcy neighborhood association, Pedro Calendario, said:

I am concerned about the future of my family and of my neighborhood. I live in the "F" area where [they] are proposing to build a park. We need a Community Benefits Agreement as a legally binding guarantee so that it can continue to exist. So that we safeguard this history and community.

---

[20] Research report on campaign contributions in Santa Brigida and neighboring communities for years 2004–2010 by the NGO SABRID.

[21] Research report on campaign contributions in Santa Brigida and neighboring communities for years 2004–2010 by the NGO SABRID, page 24.

[22] Research report on the participatory democratic process regarding the Marcy neighborhood by the NGO SABRID, page 10.

Pedro and his group, together with the SABAH coalition, saw the Santa Brigida City Hall meeting as their last chance to influence the vote. Eric Young, a SABAH coalition member, explained the key demand of the two organizations:

We want a Community Benefits Agreement, a CBA. A CBA is a contract signed by the city, the community, and the developer, and it requires the developer to provide specific amenities so that a measurable benefit is being made to the neighborhood, and such agreements have been made by cities used all over the country. It means that the city officials commit to stay true to the ten-years' redevelopment plan including affordable housing and a park, among other things. It's a cutting-edge [agreement] to honor the voice of the community.[23]

Eric is the director of SABRID,[24] an NGO that is a part of the SABAH coalition. Eric and his nonprofit organization have assisted cities implementing urban development projects all across California. According to Eric, a Community Benefits Agreement would include antidisplacement provisions for current residents as well as secure future employment opportunities.

Leading up to the final meeting and during the meeting itself, city staffers working on the redevelopment project seemed reluctant to engage in direct dialogue and share information with residents. In particular, they were unwilling to share information on the environmental sustainability of the project. Anita, a SABAH community organizer, complained:

The EIR [*Environmental Impact Report*] is a very technical and legal document, and it did NOT sufficiently consider environmental issues. Then, also, it gets translated by city council translators who often mess up Spanish.

City staffers admitted – as per this city staffer's comment at the final city hall meeting – that their final Environmental Impact Report had not yet been distributed to citizens prior to the meeting:

The EIR, that is, the Environmental Impact Report, answers all questions asked by citizens, and we will also continue in the future to answer all questions that you have. The final EIR has not yet been distributed to citizens.[25]

Maria Silva and other affected residents who had participated in the official participatory urban-planning process were not only frustrated that city staffers did not communicate relevant information; they were also in urgent need of affordable housing. They supported the proposal of a Community Benefits Agreement and had shown up at city hall that night to express this.

Maria was a retired schoolteacher directly affected by the planned redevelopment project. She had recently migrated to Santa Brigida from Mexico to support her daughter by taking care of her grandchildren. At the

---

[23] My interview, Santa Brigida, June 18, 2010.

[24] SABRID's official mission was to "bring workers, families and community partners together to organize and advocate for good jobs, strong neighborhoods and an inclusive democracy."

[25] My fieldnotes, Santa Brigida City Hall meeting, June 7, 2010.

meeting Maria described the urgency of her family's need for more affordable housing and her frustration about the city's plan to destroy the old buildings, in one of which she currently lived:

I live in the area that is going to be developed. I take care of my grandchildren. We pay $1,000 for a one-bedroom apartment, and the owners [lock] us out when the children play in the yard. They're going to demolish these houses; we need the city council's help, we need a CBA. If you are going to do something, why not write it down? We support the project, but we need guarantees.[26]

Feeling more comfortable expressing her demands in Spanish rather than in English, Maria had initially welcomed the presence of Daniel Bueno and bilingual council members who had originally shown their openness to agreeing to sign a legally binding Community Benefits Agreement (CBA) with the community and the developer but then had withdrawn from their initial promise. In Maria's speech, she asked for written "guarantees," referring to the agreement that she urged city council members to sign. From the residents' perspective, the CBA would provide greater security to those who were about to lose their current apartments, as it contained a legally binding guarantee that the city would actually provide a sufficient number of affordable housing units – as promised by the developer. Clearly, it was Daniel Bueno and his colleagues whom Maria and other residents were addressing in their speeches during the decisive city hall meeting.

Last, SABAH community organizer Anita was dismayed about the mayor's and other city council members' facilitation style:

They organize it in a way so that developers come to speak first and have unlimited time for presentation. We, the community, get a somewhat reduced physical space through the way the spatial setting is organized, like you saw at city hall, and our time for comments is reduced as well.[27]

Indeed, the mayor gave 90 percent of the available discussion time over to city council members, city planners, and urban developers, reserving only 10 percent of the time – a total of thirty minutes, for the residents affected by the project to "ask questions" with the implication that statements and opinions were not welcome. The first two hours were in effect dedicated to praising his administration's work in different areas of policy, including budgeting and public services. As time wore on, citizens began to boo at the mayor, who seemed to artificially delay the meeting to discourage participation.

Behind me, wearing blue jeans and a dark leather jacket, sat Eduardo Sanchez and his wife, Andrea: grocery shop owners who would be affected by the redevelopment project and its planned large-scale commercial shops competing with their small neighborhood business. This was not Eduardo's

---

[26] My fieldnotes, Santa Brigida City Hall meeting, June 7, 2010.
[27] My interview with an SABAH organizer, Santa Brigida, June 18, 2010.

first meeting, and as I asked him for the time, he started to explain some of his previous experiences. Bending over to my bench, he whispered:

The problem here in Santa Brigida is that the mayor won't listen to the people. That's why we're here. They've put our opportunity to speak up tonight at the end of the meeting so that the meeting takes so long so that we people will have to leave. Do you see those people behind? They have small children.

Eduardo pointed to the back of the assembly room, close to the door, where many residents were lined up, explaining that they did not speak English; they were using simultaneous interpretation provided by city officials. I saw thirty young women in their twenties and thirty older women in their forties and fifties, many looking tired. A dozen women held babies in their arms. Most were poor, Spanish-speaking immigrants. Among them I spotted Maria Silva, who had tried to voice her claims before, along with many of her neighbors.

At 7:00 p.m., two hours after the start of the meeting, the mayor finally opened the discussion for residents to "comment" on what had been said so far. Outraged about what they saw as an intentional delay, a handful of residents and some members of local civic associations lined up in front of the microphone at the back of the assembly. The mayor reacted to residents' statements in an authoritarian style by interrupting them and addressing them with their first names as in the following scene.

Gustavo Garuda, presenting himself as a "proud" US citizen of Mexican descent, approached the microphone. He said he was eager to support city council's approach to "law and order," but criticized the mayor's proposal to hire a for-profit development firm to carry out the planning project. His voice rose, and the mayor interrupted him. Notably deepening his own voice, he spoke loudly: "Gustavo, can you PLEASE calm down." Before Gustavo could respond, the mayor interrupted him, again using his first name: "Come to an end, Gustavo." Gustavo's speech had not taken longer than two minutes in total.

Rubio Paloma, a local businessman, then rose and spoke calmly, Eduardo and other residents leaning forward to hear him. Community women in the back were wearing headphones for simultaneous interpretation. He began:

I am Rubio Paloma; you all know me. I did not want to speak up, and I will only speak briefly. This here reminds me of a city council meeting forty years ago, when my neighbors and my parents wanted a park, and the city council then used exactly the same strategy as you do here today – let people wait for long hours and let them speak only at the very end of the meeting – and they decided against us. I feel caught in a bad movie by the fact that this city council here today is using exactly the same strategy as they used forty years ago. You act as if we were simply not here. At the time [forty years ago] they let people wait, because they knew they had small children and had to go home. My parents told me, Rubio, you need to be a leader. I came here because I just wanted to see how the discussion goes. Now I feel like I'm sitting in a bad movie. I wanted [dialogue] but now I know [the city council] does not want to [hear our voices]. I tell you that now we're gonna have some action around the city.

This testimony was met with huge applause from the assembly. The mayor again responded calmly:

I think people need to calm down a little. This is not a campaign race. I apologize for the confusion. We need more respect for Santa Brigida City Council personnel who have done all this work. I interrupt the meeting for a fifteen-minute break.

He left the room, followed by the entire city council. Two minutes later, three police officers approached Gustavo, the first speaker. They shouted at him in English and checked his identity. Residents who had remained seated started shouting, daring the police officers: "Go ahead, throw him out!" Ignoring these protests, the uniformed police continued to question Gustavo, who remained seated for several minutes. Although they allowed him to stay, their action served as a warning to other participants: this meeting was being harshly policed.

After the break, the Mayor Peña restarted the debate by implying that Rubio Paloma had disrespected the staff:

I ask everybody to please respect the staff presentation of our budget plans. Everything here is totally transparent. Every report discussed during the evening has been translated into Spanish, and all citizens have been given insight into it.

Samantha Clark, a bilingual council member, then backed up the mayor:

I think that respect is very important, and Francisco Rutierez's [staffer] work was disrespected in that manner. We have to respect our staff. They just do their work and they must be allowed to give long presentations. I ask those who did not listen to you, Francisco, to apologize after the end of the meeting, and if they do it not, I will apologize for them. Thank you, Francisco.

Progressive City Councilor Daniel Bueno, awkwardly rubbing his tie, agreed: "Yes, really, that wasn't respectful at all. We are a great city; we work together, be together, and we'll do it." Sal Tijolero, the council member most critical of the mayor, remained silent.

POLITICAL TRANSLATORS' EMBEDDED INTERESTS
IN INSTITUTIONAL POWER

Of the three progressive council members, Sal Tijolero was the only one who had not applauded the mayor's punitive interruption of the meeting and his involvement of the police. During a break in the meeting, Sal Tijolero informally approached SABAH community organizers to apologize to local residents for the harsh interventions by the mayor and police officers.[28]

---

[28] My fieldnotes, Santa Brigida City Hall meeting, June 7, 2010.

Then, minutes into the meeting, Natasha Nash, City Council Executive Manager, delivered a PowerPoint presentation with the final plan for the redevelopment project. Fewer than half of the slides had been translated into Spanish. She turned her back to the local residents in attendance, giving the impression that she was speaking only to council members. Nash spoke defensively:

We have engaged in serious negotiations with SABIS, I am sorry, with SABAH. You know [*addresses the city council*] that [SABAH] wanted to impede [the project] from the very beginning, that you won't have development. And you know how we tried to address the claims made by SABAH. SABAH said, for example, that we would simply displace people from their houses before we had found new houses for them. But our plan offers seventy-four units, and all are affordable housing, $900 monthly for two-bedroom apartments, while the market rent is about $1,300 per month. And 20 percent of the units are under $600 ... We also have a written statement here, which explains why the benefits of the project outweigh the identified environmental impacts ... The project, in terms of benefits, will allow new public transport ... [and] affordable housing ... and [create] a more walkable neighborhood. The alternative to the proposed project would be that there is no project, which means no development.

Nash's statement expressed a distant or even hostile relationship by city council staffers toward the neighborhood coalition SABAH. Although progressive city council members did not approve of city staffers' attitude and behavior toward residents in meetings, they did not intervene. At an earlier informal community meeting, Sal Tijolero had talked about the relationship between city staffers and new elected Latino/a council members. His comment, although vague, hints at the implicit power hierarchy and the informal and formal influence of the staffers regarding the final decision at city hall: "Things are complicated in Santa Brigida. We need the [redevelopment] project. At the city council, there are so many persons, there are rites. It is racist. But you can trust us."[29] Tijolero's remark also points to another implicit string attached to the project: several of the more conservative council members had a conflict of interest in the form of private investments that would benefit from the redevelopment project.

But the bombshell was in rumors circulating during the final city hall meeting among residents. Eduardo whispered to me: "Samantha Clark doesn't say that her election campaign has actually been funded by the development company, and they don't want the affordable housing plan." The fact that at least one of the city council members who desired to serve the lower-income and immigrant members of the community was politically beholden to the commercial developers who contributed significantly to council members' campaigns became public following the meeting.[30] The fact that also one of the progressive council

---

[29] My fieldnotes, SABAH Community meeting, Santa Brigida, June 2, 2010.

[30] *Santa Brigida News*, September 14, 2010, based on Clark's campaign financing report from June 30, 2010. The report was confirmed by a second source: a research report on campaign contributions in Santa Brigida and neighboring communities for years 2004–2010 by the NGO SABRID, page 24.

members, Clark, had been funded by the for-profit development company put at stake her credibility and political legitimacy as a representative.

The management director of the development company, Bill King, stated:

We are not consultants. We're not coming up with another plan. We're coming to implement this one, and it will be affordable. Whatever happens here today, we are going to continue to talk to the community. Housing is at the center. We tried not to maximize density, which was a conscious decision so that we have more space. It was a decision in dialogue with the community. We are coming to implement this plan, and it will be affordable.

With this statement, the developer signaled that the plan was already a fait accompli, no point in protesting it, and that nobody need question whether the housing it provided would be "affordable." However, the developer did also signal his interest in further "talk to the community," and he seemed, at least publicly, more open to dialogue with local residents than did the city staffers.

AN OPENING FOR POLITICAL TRANSLATION: MAYOR PEÑA LEAVES THE ASSEMBLY

About three hours into the meeting, at 8:00 p.m., the mayor unexpectedly left the assembly. Two other city council members grandly announced that they, too, must leave early, explaining that they had property assets in the area of the development project and would therefore abstain from voting. This surprise exit, although procedurally legitimate, palpably increased the sentiment of frustration.

Daniel Bueno, Samantha Clark, and Sal Tijolero were now left alone with approximately one hundred fifty residents who remained. They also now had a majority of votes on the redevelopment project. Sal Tijolero took the microphone and made an announcement that generated hope for improved community dialogue during the remainder of the meeting. Sal Tijolero said:

Three people [*the mayor and two city council members*] who did not know how long it would take left this meeting. I want to apologize from the bottom of my heart. I know this is a [procedural] tactic [on the part of the mayor, who controlled the meeting agenda to discourage people's participation], but this is not on our intention.

Diego Gonzalez, the mayor pro tem and a close political ally to the mayor, then arose from the audience and assumed the position of meeting facilitator. Gonzalez's web page presents his pride in using his expertise in budgetary and economic policy to save the city from bankruptcy. He announced

"You have heard, we don't accept comments on the development project now."
"What?" [*Voices rise in surprise at this further delay.*]

Not until an hour and a half later, at 9:30 p.m., was the first resident finally given permission to ask questions on the redevelopment project's environmental sustainability. However, only residents who had submitted written comments earlier were permitted to speak, with the restriction that these comments must directly relate to the Environmental Impact Report itself. Because the report had been written in technical, legalistic language, this constituted an implicit procedural hurdle. The first speaker was a resident and a member of the Santa Brigida chapter of LULAC (The League of United Latin American Citizens), a Latino/a antidiscrimination organization.[31] He said, in Spanish:

I'm totally dissatisfied. As LULAC, we wrote proposals on the Environmental Impact Report. You did not adequately answer our three major concerns. Our third concern regards issues of climate change. For four years we talk to you and it goes back and forth, these inconsistencies. The plan presented here is totally inconsistent, unclear ... Some of the things in the report are simply not correct. What we are concerned about and permanently addressed are the toxic substances ... You want to allow for toxic [contamination]. And the State of California and the City of Rockhill agree that the project at its present state [does not sufficiently consider] the issue of potential toxic substances. Their point is the same argument as ours, which is, that it [is not sustainable but dangerous].

The three progressive council members remained silent. The LULAC speaker continued, "The City of Rockhill and many other voices say that it is too fast. We oppose a project that does not conform with environmental standards." As the speaker continued, Facilitator Gonzalez commented: "Please keep with your three minutes, otherwise I turn off your microphone!"

Gonzalez interrupted the speaker another three times, yet as he concluded, there was huge applause for the first time in two hours.

Why did the city council members who held the role of institutional political translators remain silent in the face of such interactions? When I put this question to Daniel Bueno, he shared his deep distrust toward local community organizations such as LULAC, which formed part of the broader SABAH coalition:

SABAH includes a long list of ten organizations, some of which I had never heard of. I didn't feel it was prudent as an elected representative to make this list of groups happy, where at any point they could turn around and sue us. You can have an executive director of an NGO living in Rockhill speaking to us, but if a woman who has small children speaks, it's not theory, it's reality.

Like the other progressive council members, Bueno feared SABAH leaders. He criticized SABAH member Eric Young, the individual he referred to as "an executive director of an NGO living in Rockhill," as lacking legitimacy. Like the mayor, institutional political translators trusted only those community development organizations that they saw as their personal allies, based on an

---

[31] LULAC is a nationwide civic association aiming to end ethnic discrimination against Latino/as in the United States. LULAC was created by several preexisting civil rights groups and by Hispanic veterans who fought in World War I. For the organization's webpage, see lulac.org.

informal exchange of votes and connections (McQuarrie 2015). Daniel Bueno's statement implied that democratic dialogue at city hall is unsuccessful because institutional political translators distrust the independent civic associations in town who saw fit to unite as the SABAH coalition for sustainable development.

However, SABAH organizers affirmed that they saw themselves not as competition but as allies to political decision-makers and that they had sought dialogue, rather than polarization, through multiple personal and public meetings. Eric Young told me in a background interview:

It wasn't a polarized situation before that meeting. I have rarely ever seen anything like this anywhere else. In other cities, the outcome of political decision-making on planning was similar, but people did not feel that disrespected as at the Santa Brigida City Council. I have done work on development projects for twenty years in Orange County and elsewhere. In L.A., where the first Community Benefits Agreement was agreed [upon], the development project has been perceived as wildly successful; it helped create new jobs there. You won't win if you won't win for everybody. Why wouldn't you take in the positions of community-based organizations before proceeding with a development plan, what's the reason not to do it? We were prepared to negotiate each of our points, but then the city stopped negotiation. If they were afraid of anything, then [*it was?*] of political repercussions. What eventually happened [*following the decision-making*] was that people sued the city. That delayed the project. It could have been avoided if they had included all stakeholders – it would have been better for everybody.

DISCOURSE ANALYSIS

The last thirty minutes of the city hall meeting were the crucial minutes for Daniel Bueno, Samantha Clark, and Sal Tijolero: the period during which they had an opportunity to listen to residents' voices unmediated and consider their concerns. In that limited amount of time, a dozen individuals stepped forward. Despite the late hour of 10:15 p.m., five hours after the beginning of the meeting, the level of attention was high. Speakers included Latino/a youth and local residents, young women with babies, and older residents. Many expressed the worry that they would lose their homes – overcrowded and overpriced as they might be – with no chance of being offered affordable replacements.

Carmen Nuñez was the first local resident to comment. She spoke loudly and clearly, making it plain that she spoke both for herself and for others in the SABAH coalition. But before she could conclude her comments, facilitator Gonzalez interrupted her in English: "I know you want to comment on the experiences of your community, but at this point, you can only make individual comments. Speak for yourself." Carmen looked taken aback, then said, in broken English: "Our people came here to make comments." Gonzalez answered "Yes, but they can talk afterwards. You need to make general comments only."

Carmen then lowered her voice and seemed to shrink into herself. Newly careful and hesitant, she began: "We want the council to take into consideration our ideas." I noted that she had trouble finding the right words in English. She cited several problems in the community, making an effort to keep them as "general" as possible, which was difficult given her subject:

We want a bridge over the [existing highway] for the children and no new highway. It is six years since my son is dead and since then I'm active for the neighborhood and I still wish that you people change something.

The facilitator and three city council members did not respond. Another resident then spoke in English:

My name is Michael, and I live in the neighborhood affected. I am here because I am afraid to walk out in my own neighborhood. It's just ignored. My frustration of this city council – you only point your fingers against each other, but you do not help us, the people! There are whole neighborhoods in flames. The police don't go in, they just let it burn. When I call the police, I have to wait three hours. And you guys say there's no money and then you license the bosses. You tell that you had negotiated and built faith. But I don't believe it. I don't think you're doing your work.

Facilitator Gonzalez interrupted the speaker: "Michael, please end." His treatment of this male, English-fluent participant was, nevertheless, clearly more congenial than the complete disregard Gonzalez and his colleagues had showed to Carmen. Moreover, the facilitator addressed some poorer participants by their first names and misspelled the family names of others. His lack of regard for local residents' comments became still more obvious when he began chatting with other council members while the residents tried to address him. Several of the speakers interrupted their own remarks to rebuke him: "Can you please listen to what I say. Apologize!"

Without responding, the facilitator asked the next speaker to come up. This speaker, a man in his fifties, introduced himself as a SABAH community organizer. He approached the microphone from the very back of the assembly, and spoke in fluent English:

I ask you to postpone the vote. You have not given any guarantee to the community. Nothing. The park is not guaranteed. We only got promises. In the same way as these promises about today's meeting. At 4:30 a.m. I have to go to work tomorrow morning, and I have children. This was really a disrespectful meeting.

The huge round of applause that followed encouraged more residents to go to the front of the line to express their demands. Among them was Maria Silva, who spoke in Spanish: "I am very frustrated. You know that we are not employees [who are paid to attend the meeting]; we are people [who have their own work and family obligations to attend to]. We have to get up early in the morning; you know this very well . . ."

The facilitator interrupted her in Spanish: "Please, Maria, get to the end of your comments."

She continued, "I am angry. It's about representation. All it takes is for you to sign the Community Benefits Agreement. Also, we're not in office; [you are our elected representatives]. Just postpone the project. Sit down with us in good faith."

Maria's comments were met with huge applause. She was urging the progressive council members to engage in direct dialogue with her and other residents, hoping they would support the Community Benefits Agreement that all civic associations, NGOs, and residents speaking in the discussion during the evening had been asking for. Yet her statement also included a warning. With her words, "we are not in office," she was saying to the elected representatives: "you do not represent us."

Maria's statement changed the atmosphere in the room. While the facilitator had succeeded in interrupting all previous Spanish-speaking participants, he failed to interrupt Maria. She had taken a *third* position, speaking in the name of many voices in the room who had not yet been heard. She was questioning the city council members' claim to represent the people and politically translate for them in the institutional realm. She pointed to the underlying issues of class and formal political status that divided the elected representatives from her and other residents ("You know that we are not employees, we are people. We have to stand up early. You know this very well").

Maria's speech met with no reaction from the council members – but, following her lead, the other residents also began to construct a collective "we" in their speeches on behalf of other community members and their families. The first of these, a young mother, also speaking in Spanish, directly addressed her sense of betrayal by institutional political translators:

I am Anna Ramirez. You [city council members] wanted to guide us. But now others control you. I remember you on our vote. And you said you wanted to change things, and that is why we now ask you to listen to us and to postpone your vote, to talk to us. We support you. I speak for my community, for my husband, for my children, for this city. They are here. [*Anna looks around, looks at the other people in the middle and back of the room; for the first time a speaker addresses the community members.*] They support you [elected representatives]. They support you. We [the SABAH coalition] are them [the community], and they support us. Many people couldn't come.

Bueno again nervously rubbed his tie. Clark and Sal Tijolero watched the clock, losing interest in the discussion. The local residents seemed to feel most betrayed by Daniel Bueno, Sal Tijolero, and Samantha Clark, who had promised to listen to them.

THE FINAL DECISION AND THE ABSENCE
OF DEMOCRATIC DIALOGUE

Shortly before midnight, the moment for a decision on the redevelopment project finally arrived. Not a single city council member had responded to the many comments and questions raised by residents. Facilitator Gonzalez first asked the city attorney to comment on the project. The attorney read a legalistic document asserting that the proposal was legal. He did not address the citizens' demands for a Community Benefits Agreement. No one addressed the residents' questions about their housing and other family needs.

After the attorney finished, another city council staffer gave a final PowerPoint presentation indicating one or two small formal corrections as she had earlier indicated wrong page numbers in the proposal – microchanges in response to an earlier comment from a resident. Maria addressed the English-speaking council staffer in Spanish, questioning the small number of affordable housing units built into the project, claiming that the number had been reduced to below what council members had previously indicated. She received no response from the staffer, who failed even to raise her head. Assuming there might be an acoustical problem, given that the facilitator and staffers sat at some distance from Maria at the front of the assembly, she tried again, raising her voice and directly addressing the presenter of the PowerPoint. The staffer continued to ignore her. Neither the facilitator nor the other three council members reacted. None provided a translation into English so that non–Spanish speakers might understand Maria's comments.

DEMOCRATIC CRISIS AS MISUNDERSTANDING: REPRESENTATIVES HIDE BETWEEN BUREAUCRATS

For democratic theorists, the positional misunderstanding featured here in the interactions between residents, city staffers, and the bilingual facilitator and other city council members illustrates a larger crisis of representative democracy even at the most grassroots, local level in Santa Brigida (della Porta 2012; Sitrin and Azzellini 2014).

The city officials then proceeded to the vote. The facilitator asked the other three: "Do all of you agree [on approving the development plan]?" All three echoed "Aye," and the facilitator pronounced the plan "Approved." Taken minutes before midnight, this final vote at city hall was the culmination of a deep and mutual positional misunderstanding between residents and their representatives. In the minutes after the vote, Daniel Bueno, a worried expression on his face, jumped to his feet, reached for the microphone, and addressed the two other members: "We have to respond. We have to respond." He then turned around to the assembly and pleads: "It's a contract on your behalf."

"No way!" someone shouted. Behind me, a baby began to cry, and another person shouted, "Vote him out!" Bueno looked nervous. He switched to Spanish: "Lo quiero felicitar (I want to celebrate this)." He speaks in what seems a forced way, attempting to answer one of the demands: "That park is not yet there; we're hoping that Latino access will come. I'm celebrating for you. Childcare, housing, schools . . . This here is so many city council members, so many people, and hours. This is a project with over a hundred affordable housing apartments. So many great units of dignity housing."

As shown in Chapters 1 and 2 for dominant group members, and as I shall show here, city council member Bueno seemed to really mean what he declared in public: he seemed to genuinely believe that citizen's voices *had* been included, while at the same time he was ignoring the legitimate concerns raised by the community throughout the meeting.

At that moment, about thirty minutes after midnight, the roughly fifty SABAH community members who remained at the meeting held up their banners reading "CBA" to express their preferred choice for a Community Benefits Agreement. They started chanting: "CBA, CBA." A resident shouted at Daniel: "For us, nothing changes. We wait for a contract. This here is respectless. There is no support for the community, the city wants to work for us, and we want a guarantee. We don't believe in empty promises, we want three signatures." The comment was met with huge applause.

However, like Daniel Bueno, the two other progressive council members, Sal Tijolero and Samantha Clark, also felt themselves misunderstood by residents and instead praised the decision they had just taken. Sal Tijolero took the microphone:

I don't get it. For the first time, Santa Brigida votes for the poorest of the poor. [*Shouts of* "Boohoo!"] I couldn't be for the Community Benefits Agreement because it's too complicated, but I'm for this project. We should celebrate that agreement. If we people had no vote, there would be no house for Carmen. Carmen would go home and nothing would have changed. Here is a city that condemns Arizona, and that has translation equipment for you.

Samantha Clark then took the microphone, loudly expressing anger over her perception that residents had misunderstood her and her colleagues:

The mayor and two city council members are not here tonight but they would be happy. It's a battle of victory for the community. I worked for you. I know it's difficult because we're not on the same stage tonight, but I want you to have faith.

Both Clark, with her comment about "complexity," and Tijolero have implied that the elected city council members know better than the residents what is good for their constituencies. Facilitator Gonzalez joined in: "You run for city councilor to make strong decisions, and this is one." As these observations document, even those who see themselves as initiating a political translation process may end up in the preconscious behavior that characterizes positional misunderstandings, where powerful groups ignore those whom they claim to empower.

As the facilitator began to recap the last points of the agenda, members of SABAH started clapping their hands rhythmically. The clapping increased in volume, drowning out his voice. Finally the SABAH members left the room, followed by many other participants and supporters. The assembly emptied quickly, leaving only city council members and staffers on the dais.

Outside, SABAH community members in red T-shirts formed a circle. Anita, a young community organizer in her twenties, who had volunteered as a linguistic interpreter/translator for Maria and other residents at the meeting, addressed the SABAH community members in Spanish:

This was not the end, but it was a day of continued struggle. And we were great. Let's be proud of ourselves because we can be proud of ourselves; we were so strong, so present; so long we fought and we stayed so long.

The SABAH community members and their supporters applauded each other in a loud and powerful moment of solidarity. Other meeting participants leaving the assembly spontaneously joined in the SABAH community members' applause.

WHY POLITICAL TRANSLATION FAILED AT CITY HALL

In Santa Brigida, three council members thought they could use their positions to "empower" residents at city hall. I was specifically interested in the "institutional political translator" role played by these progressive city council members, who saw themselves not only as representatives of those communities but as true advocates for their communities. All of them wanted "dialogue" in their community but, by the end of this polarizing meeting, were shouted down as "liars" by their electorate. As all three admitted, their embedded institutional power position was the source of the deepening misunderstanding with residents. Daniel Bueno, Samantha Clark, and Sal Tijolero had gradually come to align their politics and interests with those of institutional elites, developers, and business industries. Indeed, one of them, Samantha Clark, was implicitly beholden, as she had even received campaign funding from the development firm involved in the project.[32] Even those city council members who did not directly owe their power to the commercial interests had come to identify with that power structure far more than with their constituents' needs – even when they shared aspects of ethnic and economic background with those constituents. This failure of institutional political translation was at the very center of the council's sometimes shockingly dismissive, patronizing, and even abusive treatment of community members at the meeting. Unlike the independent political translators discussed in other chapters, these city council members had seen themselves as representatives as well as constituents of the people in the meeting, yet by *becoming* representatives, they had apparently "cut off" their own capacity to listen to those who had trusted in them. Political translation had turned into representation and domination.

---

[32] This information is confirmed by three different sources. First, it is confirmed by a research report on campaign contributions in Santa Brigida and neighboring communities for the years 2004–2010 by the NGO SABRID (see pages 10–11 and 24). Second, it is confirmed by reports on Clark's case by the local *Santa Brigida News* from Sept 14, 2010. Third, the *Santa Brigida Gazette* documents two contributions by the development firm and its director, based on Clark's public campaign finance reports for April and June of 2010.

4

Santa Brigida Revisited

A week before the contentious open meeting with the Santa Brigida city councilors, many of the immigrant residents had met in another forum, this one organized by the Santa Brigida Alliance for Affordable Housing (SABAH) coalition. SABAH and its organizers were committed to building a communicative space for radical democracy that would interrupt the institutionalized power structure and bring immigrant voices more authentically into city government.

I have dubbed the SABAH key group of organizers – many of them first- and second-generation immigrants – *community* political translators, because they acted as an intermediary third between residents and sympathetic city council members. These organizers did not want to acquire individual positions of power at city hall. They formed part of what they saw as an urban social movement protesting against the neoliberal conditions of inequality in the aftermath of the 2008 financial crisis (Mayer 2009b, 2012; McQuarrie 2015; Nichols and Uitermark 2016; Smith and Wiest 2012; Smith 2017). Based on their backgrounds in Latino/a and Chicano/a community education, they saw themselves as engaged in a long-term "intentional" grassroots education project connected to the struggle for immigrants' rights (Anzaldúa 1999; Guerrero 2010; Ganz and Lin 2011; Juris 2013; Zepeda-Millán 2016; Nichols and Uitermark 2016). The Community Forum they designed put Spanish-speaking residents at the center of the conversation, vesting them with the power and authority to criticize and suggest alternatives to the city-planning proceedings in ways that had been impossible in earlier city hall meetings, and that would be severely tested in the one on June 7. Although the city council ultimately voted against the key demand made by this group, SABAH's Community Forum and the coalition's critical political translation tactics resulted in significant concessions from city council members and empowered Santa Brigida residents to take part in the deliberative process.

The June 2 SABAH Community Forum did not represent a dialogue-oriented, consensus-based civic forum but rather an adversarial context for political negotiation between mainstream politicians and immigrant residents

(Mische 2008). As a hybrid forum for democratic communication involving representative and deliberative elements, the SABAH forum enabled residents to assume a collective leadership position. By acting as meeting chairs and facilitators at the SABAH forum, immigrant residents who had previously been absent from city government confronted elected representatives with the wishes of their constituencies. By doing little more than taking a third-party witnessing position during proceedings, SABAH community translators helped disadvantaged community members to negotiate face to face with their elected representatives.

As used by local community organizers in Santa Brigida, political translation made it possible for socially disadvantaged residents and immigrants to become collective speakers on behalf of their communities, without being formally elected. Democratic theorists have only recently started to acknowledge that the distinction between representative democracy (based on elections) and radical/participatory democracy is somewhat artificial (Plotke 1997; Mansbridge 2003; Urbinati 2000; Urbinati and Warren 2008). At the June 2 SABAH forum, residents spoke both for themselves and for others as a collective. Created originally as a response to the failed official meetings on the redevelopment project, the SABAH forum established itself from 2010 onwards as an alternative public venue, lending public visibility to residents' positions on a range of policy issues including health care and policing of undocumented immigrants. The forum also mobilized residents to attend official city hall meetings to voice dissent and participate in protest actions. It was a great success for SABAH to persuade city council members to participate in their forum meetings on a regular basis.

BUILDING THE SABAH COMMUNITY FORUM: IMMIGRANTS AS POLITICAL TRANSLATORS

Anita Garcia is one of the SABAH community organizers who put together the SABAH Community Forum. She and some colleagues who had previously volunteered for linguistic translation at the city hall meetings had become aware of the many ways in which standard meeting protocols marginalized the voices of many immigrant residents. They devised the SABAH forum to give residents and their communities a public platform from which to speak and criticize, and to train them to interact with city council members and more established local associations, including churches. She explained to me:

People prefer to talk to elected representatives in our spaces – for example, in a meeting we organized at a local community church. Translation is so hard to do! At the city council, they usually have that man [official city council interpreter], but if it's a meeting with the SABAH coalition, they ask me [to translate], because the residents want me to do it and the council interpreter messes up with Spanish.[1]

---

[1] My interview, June 18, 2010.

Born in Mexico, in her early twenties when these meetings took place, Anita was one of the youngest members of the SABAH organizing coalition. She and most of her SABAH colleagues grew up in Santa Brigida as members of the marginalized communities for whom they now translate. Unlike many of the more recent immigrants and undocumented workers in Santa Brigida, Anita was able to attend college – the first in her family to do so. Inspired by Chicana youth activism in her community, she chose to work as a grassroots educator and organizer for the SABAH coalition after graduating from college.

Like the other SABAH organizers, Anita had no direct personal interest in seeking elected office. This was perhaps one of the reasons why, according to Anita, the Spanish-speaking residents trusted her and other SABAH volunteer linguistic translators more than they did the official city council interpreter, whom the mayor had hired to provide simultaneous interpretation. Compared to trained, professional simultaneous interpreters, community translators are generally at the lowest end of the pay hierarchy, and those who interpret for minorities and immigrants often receive little or no pay for their work (Inghilleri 2012). In the case of Santa Brigida, community translators drew on their intrinsic commitment to and knowledge of the communities for whom they translated. Their experience in protest and community organizing vested these translators with a repertoire of political uses for their volunteer role and disruptive interventions on behalf of marginalized community members. Professional translators, trained to remain neutral, generally refuse that advocacy role (Inghilleri 2012).

In this case, SABAH volunteer translators declared that the alternative Community Forum they had organized would be chaired and conducted by the immigrant residents directly affected by decisions made at city hall. Officially, Anita and her colleagues acted as linguistic translators in this alternative forum, using their assistive position to encourage local residents to take an active role. Because of their efforts, local monolingual Spanish-speaking Latino/a residents who had been marginalized in official deliberations became key negotiators in the SABAH Community Forum.

The SABAH forum acquired power in part because it flew under the radar of political players, including the very council members and official city staffers who attended the forum. Organizers' interventions went almost unnoticed as volunteer linguistic community translators. But by changing informal role hierarchies and allowing disruptive interventions in the role of the *witnessing third party*, this collective political translation method dramatically changed the tenor of the deliberations, since no facilitator or official interrupted residents' speeches. As a result, the residents were able to compel city officials to agree to several demands.

BACKSTAGE: SETTING UP THE FORUM

Santa Brigida's SABAH Community Forum usually met before and after the official city hall meetings. As at city hall, some of the forum meetings included open debates between residents and representatives and ended with a vote on ongoing urban policy. But unlike the city hall meetings, the forum allowed voting by the residents themselves, and the city council members in attendance promised to take into consideration these collective votes when making formal decisions at city hall. Although the final vote at the SABAH forum was not legally binding, representatives saw the forum as an important public venue for additional outreach and dialogue with their voters and constituencies.

In an interview after the contentious city hall meeting of July 7, Anita told me how much effort had gone into bringing the community into the forum:

We could just *say* the SABAH forum is open, but if we're not going to be intentional, without outreach, it will not be open, [and] the same is true for the community meetings we organize with developers and council members on development. My concern is [that] we need to intentionally build relationships, a sense of community. We know how to do it and why. When I was fifteen, I first used it at La Casa de Cultura y Artes,[2] because La Casa is a place where people can become politicized – but it does not just happen naturally. The result is public access.[3]

Anita Garcia and many of her co-organizers had been trained at La Casa, a local community center that specializes in Chicano/a community organizing and grassroots education. Several SABAH organizers had also been linguistic translators in official city hall meetings and understood that city council members perceived experienced social movement activists, such as NGO staffers or Latino/a civic association leaders, as potential threats. The council members were more receptive to dialogue with community members. Accordingly, Anita and her fellow organizers trained some of these residents to become voices on behalf of community residents at the SABAH forum. Their training and "intentional" community education approach (cf. Juris 2013) formed part of a larger *political* practice of translating on behalf of their communities. Anita describes how SABAH used outreach work to build independent leadership within the community – as in the case of Maria Silva's contributions at city hall. Anita told me how important Maria had become in SABAH:

Maria is a newcomer in local politics here in Santa Brigida, whom we met through outreach work, and she has become one of the moderators for the SABAH Community Forum. [She is] one of our strongest speakers, even though she only recently immigrated to the US, and she is mainly monolingual in Spanish. That's intentional.[4]

In Anita's perception, her engagement combined linguistic translation for immigrant residents and community members with a *political* struggle for education and empowerment. In the view of mainstream politicians in Santa

[2] My interview, Santa Brigida, June 18, 2010.   [3] My interview, Santa Brigida, June 18, 2010.
[4] My interview, Santa Brigida, June 18, 2010.

Brigida, however, she was first of all a community organizer specializing in Latino/a outreach and cultural community education. Anita had an intrinsic, local connection to residents and knowledge of the Latino/a and immigrant communities that made her and her fellow translators attractive cultural intermediaries for city council members. Unnoticed by the city council members, Anita and her SABAH team self-consciously used their multilingual cultural capital and knowledge as a grassroots political strategy to empower residents. Anita described the process:

As community organizer, I try to reach out to identify grassroots leaders and build a coalition with them through the SABAH network. In 2006, SABAH felt we needed residents to codecide with us on all issues. It was a very intentional outreach, from door to door. Maria is our model case. Maria has her experience from Mexico, where she organized around schools. She is very passionate and continues to be active [after the meeting at city council].[5]

The strong position that Maria Garcia and other Spanish-speaking resident immigrants assumed at the SABAH forum had been carefully crafted with the team of community translators. Although community translators like Anita meant to empower residents by "intentionally" making them the voices of their own communities, they first had to overcome a local political history in which resident immigrants such as Maria Garcia, the "model case" for a community leader, had repeatedly been silenced and disciplined by city council members and official facilitators during city hall meetings. Another hurdle was that many residents feared the officials' unpredictable and often authoritarian interactions with the residents during meetings. As in the June 7 meeting, for example, the mayor had called upon the police to enter and discipline those residents who had spoken out against his position.

SABAH's biggest achievement was not an immediate policy outcome but the empowering of residents from disenfranchised and underrepresented groups. Because Maria was monolingual in Spanish, she could serve as a model for other resident immigrants in the community to speak their minds in public, even if they were not fluent in English. Anita explains:

It is also for Maria's grandchildren. It is an example for them seeing her be active, which has motivated them to speak up in class. That's exactly what our model wants. It's this impact in terms of development and decision-making, that those who are affected by decision-makers have access to politics.[6]

HIDDEN LEVERAGE

In addition to attracting and empowering residents, SABAH took the parallel step of "intentional" outreach toward city council members and officials – mainstream

---

[5] My interview, Santa Brigida, June 18, 2010.   [6] My interview, Santa Brigida, June 18, 2010.

actors in institutional politics. Anita and her team had realized that their officially accredited role as volunteer translators gave them the unique leverage to set up an egalitarian forum for political negotiation in an adversarial political context. This kind of outreach to officials was strategic. It taught city council members to engage in an "intentional," more respectful, and more egalitarian relationship with community members. Anita explained:

The intention is to get people [who are] affected and then you do an intentional outreach. Intentionality means also to negotiate with each single council member. We first talked to each separately, and we also taught city staffers on the intentional approach. Then we had three public meetings with developers, city council members, and staffers.[7]

The SABAH community translators got the city councilors to attend their forum in the name of grassroots education. The councilors' decision to participate in the Community Forum then became a source of informal power for the entire SABAH coalition.

Given city council members' outspoken expression of mistrust toward the SABAH coalition, it was a significant achievement for SABAH's team of community translators to persuade city council members to enter into a continuous democratic dialogue in these meetings. Their youth, volunteer status, and relative inexperience with institutional city politics disarmed the councilors and made them more open to hearing the residents. The SABAH Community Forum meeting on June 2, 2010, only five days before the controversial Santa Brigida City Hall meeting, exemplifies this process.[8]

CHANGING ROLES WITHIN THE MEETING

"Hello, welcome, *buenas tardes*, thanks so much for coming! *Muchas gracias de venir!*" Maria Silva and Anita Garcia opened the forum meeting together with three other SABAH members. At first sight, the opening of the SABAH forum about urban redevelopment looked much like a city hall meeting. It brought together the same political groups and individuals, but it symbolically reversed some of the formal hierarchies and linguistic, gendered, and spatial marginalizing practices so apparent at city hall.

At city hall the mayor or the mayor pro tem presided over meetings. These facilitators repeatedly interrupted, disciplined, marginalized, and implicitly stigmatized residents who spoke, particularly Spanish-speaking participants. At the SABAH Community Forum, however, the meeting facilitators were themselves resident immigrants. This simple strategy meant that none of the elected Latino/a representatives could claim to speak on behalf of local residents.

[7] My interview, Santa Brigida, June 18, 2010.
[8] My fieldnotes, SABAH Community meeting, June 2, 2010.

The SABAH community translators also abolished the spatial hierarchies they had observed at city hall meetings. At the back door of the community meeting, hours before the meeting itself commenced, SABAH organizers began welcoming participants and distributing headphones to those who needed simultaneous interpretation. As a location for their forum, SABAH organizers had selected St. Joseph's School, a church-affiliated community school central to the neighborhood affected by the redevelopment project now under discussion. The meeting room slowly filled with about two hundred partici-pants, mostly Spanish-speaking Latino community members. They included many elderly residents who were not present at the official city hall meeting five days later. The young bilingual community organizers invited women with small children, ladies in their sixties and seventies, and other adults to seat themselves in the front of the hall. They had also organized childcare in another room. Anita told me:

When you go into their space [city hall], their representatives sit in this elevated way, on chairs that are distant to people, and they limit your time for commenting on the project. It is so structured! Also, the official participatory meetings preceding the decision at city council and organized by the development planning commission marginalized the resi-dents who had been invited to attend.[9]

In contrast, the SABAH Community Forum felt like an inclusive and safe space, enabling residents to interact with officials freely and without fear. Finding a seat at one side of the assembly, I saw city council members Daniel Bueno, Sal Tijolero, and Samantha Clark enter the meeting. These were the three pro-gressive council members who remained at the city council meeting five days later, after their colleagues had departed, but would nevertheless fail to respond to residents' questions about the redevelopment project.

DIFFERENCES IN TIME MANAGEMENT AND AGENDA SETTING

The forum began at the end of the workday, around 6:00 p.m., and ended two hours later, early enough to allow parents to put their children to bed. Anita and her team had choreographed a series of steps to encourage local residents to speak, starting with strategic scheduling decisions. In contrast, at the June 7 city hall meeting, official facilitators would use their agenda-setting power to marginalize their political foes, intentionally delaying the period for residents to speak until the very end of the meeting. This tactic produced a meeting that lasted six hours, from 5:00 p.m. to midnight. Convenient timing is particularly relevant for enhancing inclusive democracy (Polletta 2002). Setting the agenda for the meeting, SABAH organizers also ensured that residents would speak first and express their demands, making it a priority, in turn, for city council members to answer them.

[9] My interview, Santa Brigida, June 18, 2010.

The assembly was packed. Four Catholic priests, who officially hosted the event at their church-affiliated school, arrived. The gathered residents at the forum were overwhelmingly Catholic and the hosting church was engaged in social justice work. The young women who were to act as translators accompanied the priests to the microphone and introduced the youngest priest, who was white, as "Padre Stuart," giving him the microphone. He welcomed all participants in both Spanish and English, receiving enthusiastic applause. He then prayed – also bilingually – for a productive meeting: "God, let us grow." The city hall meeting would also start with an official prayer, but one given by the mayor. Here, Padre Stuart refrained from assuming an official position as facilitator, instead handing over the microphone to SABAH's Anita, who then passed it to Maria Silva (the "model case" of an involved resident) and Roberto Hernandez, another immigrant resident, introducing these two community members as the evening's official facilitators. These simple symbolic acts gave Roberto and Maria the authority to assume a public leadership position. Maria led the discussion while Roberto translated her statements into English. Maria's actions and demeanor here stood in sharp contrast to her being silenced later by the facilitator at city hall. Throughout the evening's discussion, Maria used her new front-and-center position as forum chair and facilitator to lead her community in persuading city council members to make concessions to their constituents. She and Roberto as cofacilitators collectively enabled residents to take ownership of the forum.

In their positions as volunteer linguistic translators, Anita and her fellow SABAH organizers retreated for the time being to the background of the debate. Only later, during the most heated negotiation phase, would they intervene to echo and support the voices of resident facilitators.

THE COGNITIVE DIMENSION OF POLITICAL TRANSLATION: RESIDENTS SPEAK FOR THEMSELVES

Political translation involves a cognitive dimension of knowledge-sharing that is key to providing transparency even before the start of deliberative processes. Knowledge sharing entails, for example, translating relevant legal documents into languages that local residents understand, so that they can speak for themselves and confront city officials effectively with their political demands. A significant barrier to Santa Brigida residents' ability to influence decision-making at city hall was the fact that knowledge about the redevelopment project was not transparently shared by officials and city council members during the officially "open" city hall meetings. In contrast, at the Community Forum meeting, the community translators prioritized civic access to information about the project. The forum began with local residents presenting knowledge acquired in the process of debating the development project during previous, officially organized participatory meetings.

Pilar Caliente, the first speaker, presented a brief report on the outcome of previous urban planning deliberations. A resident of the area affected by the planned redevelopment project, Pilar had attended many meetings on the project over a period of three years. In Spanish, she reported to the community what local residents had worked out together in the meetings about the project: "This is what we did in the last eight months ... This was the first step ... the second ... the third." After translating her report into English, she summed up the key difference between the proposal for urban redevelopment put forth by the City of Santa Brigida and the proposal by the group of residents who had attended all previous meetings on the topic:

In sum, this discussion today is important for all of us. It is important that we negotiate and talk with a lot of people, fight for our rights, and negotiate with the City of Santa Brigida, that we discuss why the CBA [Community Benefits Agreement] is required, what it would change, and why a Memorandum of Understanding, the so-called MoU, as city officials currently propose, is not enough to guarantee our rights. In fact, the memorandum would not be legally binding or guarantee that the city keeps its promises to the community. Thank you.

In order to allow different sets of expertise to shape the cognitive content of deliberation, SABAH co-organizers at the Community Forum asked residents to present their knowledge regarding the redevelopment project before the staffers and development-company managers gave their official reports.

At this point, Pilar as a resident expert compared two proposals on how to include affordable housing within the planned redevelopment project. One proposal, preferred by the City of Santa Brigida, emphasized options for affordable housing through a legally nonbinding Memorandum of Understanding (MoU). The second proposal, put forth by residents who had attended previous meetings on urban development and the SABAH coalition, entailed establishing a Community Benefits Agreement (CBA), a legally binding agreement between the city and the development company to guarantee benefits for the community in the form of affordable housing (see Chapter 3).

By giving residents the chance to act and speak as experts, community translators consciously allowed those affected by urban development to give voice to their communities. According to Anita:

We invest in core groups of residents to help them understand how policy is made, how the city is structured, so that they have that knowledge for themselves, to be part of decision-making because that is different from someone else talking or negotiating on their behalf.[10]

Following Anita's report, facilitators Maria and Roberto invited a city council staffer working on urban planning to provide the city government's

[10] My interview, Santa Brigida, June 18, 2010.

perspective on the project. The staffer was welcomed with applause, but she presented the report in technical language, including many abstract-sounding terms, just as she would at city hall five days later. She spoke in English, and Roberto softly intervened: "I have to translate," he reminded her.

While translating from English into Spanish, Roberto consciously extended the staffer's information by offering additional explanations for the meaning of specialized terminology, including key terms like "MoU," which she had not provided. He spoke vividly, and his translation picked up the emotional nuances in the city staffer's report, including her enthusiasm for a park. Roberto explicitly mimicked the speaker's rhythm, helping listeners to synchronize emotional attention and cognitive understanding (Collins 2005). While he spoke, other SABAH team members handed out documents in Spanish that had been provided by the staffer.

Roberto's engaged Spanish translation made it possible for community members to make sense of the different claims concerning the redevelopment project. To help them, he reframed, explained, and recontextualized the official information. Roberto's translation had a visible effect on many participants, who followed his gestures and applauded in response to parts of the report they welcomed. As a result, following Roberto's translation, the staffer switched from English to Spanish and directly addressed the audience – in complete contrast to her later behavior at city hall. At the end of the staffer's report and Roberto's translation, many residents applauded the staffer. In comparison, at city hall, when the very same staffer presented the same report at city hall, none of the Latino/a residents who listened to the simultaneous interpretation applauded.

Anita explained that both residents in general and her team of community translators found their most challenging task to be to "convey the same emotion" across cultural, formal, and linguistic hierarchies:

As a translator, I try to convey the same emotion. It's especially more important if it's from Spanish into English, because it would be horrible if it would become dry. But in other moments of debate, you can also get into a more monotonous tone. We do it automatically; both are possible.[11]

Anita's team had two groups of community translators. The first included Anita and other second-generation immigrants, who were paid by the SABAH coalition for their community organizing to set up the SABAH forum and maintain it through outreach. The second group, trained by these community organizers, included other bilingual immigrants, such as Roberto, who over time acquired sophisticated knowledge and skill as bilingual meeting facilitators, mediators, and linguistic translators. At the SABAH forums, both groups interpreted linguistically, but also translated across different forms and

[11] My interview, Santa Brigida, June 18, 2010.

formats of knowledge to make dialogue possible and to convey meanings across cultural differences. All of these practices helped in creating "public access," as Anita describes it.

Democratic theorists have categorized such complex intercultural translating practices as essential to deliberation in culturally diverse or multilingual settings (Nanz 2006).

After the two reports by a resident and a city staffer, the discussion itself began. For one hour, residents, city staffers and urban developers offered comments. Most residents spoke in Spanish, while city staffers and urban developers responded in English. In addition to the consecutive interpretation by community translators into Spanish, simultaneous interpretation was made available by volunteers for English speakers. The facilitators then invited various groups to share their opinions on the report, stressing the oral form of "testimonies." Many Spanish-speaking residents, encouraged by Roberto's translation of the official report, expressed their passion about the debate. They spoke loudly, clearly and proudly – in contrast to their shy, hesitant speeches and fearful body language at city council meetings.

Carmen Nuñez delivered the first testimony. She stood to be affected by the planned destruction of historical Marcy District houses proposed in the redevelopment plan. In her testimony, delivered entirely in Spanish, she recounted how she and others started the SABAH coalition to change something about their situation. Her testimony emphasized the joint struggle and solidarity among "comrades and friends:"

Buenas tardes compañeros y amigos ... [*English translation:*] I am Carmen Nuñez, I live in Eighteenth Street. In my daily life, I would need a lot of things to improve. Things are not easy to get [and] too expensive where I live. For example, bread is not easy to get where I live, and there are a lot of people in the street who drink; there is drugs, a lot of young guys. That's not ideal for my children. There is the struggle about drugs. That is how we friends [*Spanish original: amigos y amigas*] came together, [joined/created SABAH]. We want the city to listen to us ... I thank all compañeros. [*Huge applause.*]

The content of the stories told by the residents in this meeting differed from that of the stories that city council members told about residents at the official city hall forum five days later. There the city council members would speak abstractly of residents' "empowerment." Here the voices of the residents and their own experiences and needs formed the starting point of the discussion in contrast to the proceedings at city hall.

Inspired by Carmen's story, several other residents made passionate statements. Maria and Roberto explicitly welcomed a variety of views on the redevelopment project. A woman in her mid-forties addressed city council members directly, asking for a political response to the Marcy neighborhood's exceedingly expensive rents, which forced many families to live together in tiny apartments:

It is unfair how we are treated by landlords in this neighborhood. How should three families live within one room? At the moment I am living in a small, expensive one-room apartment, so that my children will have the chance to study ... Therefore we need an all-Latino city council.

A trade-union organizer in his mid-twenties, who sat next to me in the assembly, responded so that all could hear: "An all-Latino city council is not enough."

More and more participants in the assembly raised banners asking for a CBA, reinforcing speakers who asked city council members and official city staffers for a political response and dialogue with residents. A man in his fifties gently interrupted the expected procedural order, saying,

If I look back [*low voice*] – for three years I have now been participating in the meetings [on the planned local urban redevelopment project]. At the beginning, things looked insecure, but then we came up with the CBA ... [*Now passionate*:] Never, never will they keep their promises to construct sufficient houses for people with low income. We have too many poor people here. They have not kept their promises in the past so why should they do it in the future. We are poor people. Without the CBA we are looking into an insecure future. [*Huge applause.*]

Although the residents did not agree with one another, many argued in favor of the CBA.

POLITICIANS RESPOND TO RESIDENTS: CONCESSIONS

Now Maria, as facilitator, summed up the residents' proposals and called upon the first of the three invited city council members, Samantha Clark, to state her position.

Clark began in Spanish, then switched to English, saying, "I am more fluent in English; I apologize." She spoke so passionately and rapidly in English that her comments were sometimes difficult to follow:

I can't stand here and be dishonest. Look, in the city council, there are only four people, four votes. [*Only four Council members could vote on the decision about the redevelopment project as the mayor and two other council members owned property in the area and had abstained* (Chapter 3).] I will do what I can [*Someone in the audience calls out*: "No!"], but I can't stop the project for the CBA. [*Someone in the audience calls in English*: "Why not?" *Someone else calls out*: "You are one vote!" *Clark switches into English.*] And after thirty years, the State of California will for the first time give a grant for a huge redevelopment project in our city. I have waited for this all my life. [*More participants call out questions in English, then someone in the audience shouts in Spanish*: "You have to keep your integrity!" *Booing and chanting start*: "CBA, CBA!"]. [*Clark continues in English*:] "I am honest!"

Clark spoke so fast that Roberto could hardly follow to translate her comments. When he tried to politely intervene to initiate a Spanish translation, Clark ignored him and continued speaking.

In stressing her integrity, Clark was trying to counter persistent rumors about her corruption.[12] She had to struggle against the fact that although she seemed initially to have supported residents' proposal for a CBA, she was now backing away.

Roberto politely interrupted Clark in English: "Excuse me, but you have not answered several concrete questions asked by people here tonight." Roberto summed up a number of points raised by residents yet not answered by Clark, then he provided a Spanish translation of his questions and asked Clark to respond to each one. He also requested that she speak more slowly so that he could translate. His intervention changed the pace of discussion to allow more interaction.

Clark immediately responded to Roberto in Spanish, but her difficulties with the language made it hard for her to explain in depth. In Spanish she said briefly, "I am sorry. We are in this complicated situation. That is why we can't [sign the CBA]." She then responded to the questions posed by several different residents, with Roberto translating.

At one point as Clark was speaking, an old man in the assembly raised his hand. She continued speaking until someone in the assembly shouted, "Abuelito, habla!" (Grandfather, talk!)

From his seat in the front row, the elderly man offered his opinion about the development project in Spanish. Clark replied, this time switching into Spanish. Someone from the assembly exclaimed in Spanish: "When you were trying to get elected, you said that you were with Latinos!" Clark responded in English: "They deserve a better future!" In response, many in the assembly broke into the chant: "CBA, CBA!"

In this situation, by politely interrupting to ask several pointed questions echoing residents' voices, Roberto transcended the classical role of a linguistic translator. Later, Anita told me that his interruption formed a key part of SABAH's community translating strategy to intervene and disrupt lengthy statements by politicians:

Translation is so hard to do! City council members such as Sal Tijolero and Samantha Clark systematically interrupt our speakers in the meetings hosted at city hall or in meetings in which developers are present ... That is why we adopted an intentional model for meetings we organize as SABAH coalition.[13]

In another example, when Clark was telling her personal story, describing her motivation to support the development project, the bilingual translators and facilitators together gently forced her to give the "Grandfather" from the floor an answer. Their goal was to create a public space that allows for the passionate

---

[12] In Chapter 3, I discuss critiques by residents and SABAH indicating that shortly before and after the final decision about the redevelopment project was made, this council member had received campaign funding from the developer.

[13] My interview, Santa Brigida, June 18, 2010.

but respectful expression of different arguments and even their accompanying emotions. The interchange also allowed community members to respond, when Clark suggested that a CBA was "too complicated" without specifying why, by starting to chant "CBA," indicating their strong disagreement with her position. The facilitators and translators from SABAH did not silence this expression of passion as the city hall facilitators would have done. The result was a lively and productive debate, given that Clark was not the only council member to respond to residents' demands.

CRITICAL INTERVENTIONS

The last forty-five minutes of the meeting produced a high-stakes negotiation in which residents attempted to gain concessions from city council members. At this decisive moment, Maria as facilitator called on city council member Sal Tijolero to speak to the assembly. Tijolero, a first-generation immigrant, was more fluent in Spanish than Clark, so the discussion proceeded at that point in Spanish. Yet Tijolero, too, tried to evade residents' criticisms of the redevelopment project. He first took credit for the new linguistic translation of the open Council meeting:

We want to say one thing: in the city council, one speaks only in English. And we said, No! Spanish interpretation is expensive, but we have provided it for you.

A man from the audience interrupted to complain about ongoing marginalization of residents at city hall meetings, and Tijolero replied,

I know there is linguistic discrimination at city hall. That's why we are there. On your behalf we have made possible language access there.

The crowd did not let him change the subject, and broke into a chant of "CBA, CBA!" Others joined in.

[*A voice from the audience call out*:] But if you were speaking for us, why did you vote like you did in the last meeting? You were there. In fact, you did not represent Latino interests. You voted with conservatives! We are [more than a hundred] people living in the houses [that will be destroyed]. They are historical houses! That is why we need a CBA! [*Again, a chorus of many voices*: "CBA, CBA!"]

After Sal Tijolero failed to answer several questions from participants in the assembly, SABAH community translator Anita intervened. She was standing next to Tijolero but used a microphone to echo and emphasize residents' questions, connecting them to Tijolero's past political positions. She said, "You had said that you would vote in favor of the CBA at city hall."

Tijolero answered briefly, "That is right."

Maria joined in the discussion, repeating arguments made by residents: "All of these proposals make clear exactly why we want a CBA ... And the majority of us want that. That is why we would like to conserve the houses for this community, as you also say you want."

Tijolero responded briefly: "It is impossible."

Resident facilitator Maria: "Sí, se puede!" (Yes, we can! – *a phrase now famous in chants and protests*).

People throughout the assembly began to chant "CBA" and to support Maria with loud, long-lasting applause.

Tijolero: "Listen, I do not agree, we cannot simply continue talking. There are constraints."

Anita: "What exactly are the constraints?" (*Huge applause.*)

Council member Tijolero then talked about his personal roots and his commitment to the area affected by the development plan. He concluded his statement by saying, "It is not easy for us to commit to a CBA given that the funding situation may change. You know all that very well."

During this sequence of events, Anita did not intervene to provide linguistic translation. Almost all of the discussion with city council members was carried out in Spanish, so linguistic translation for the residents was unnecessary. Anita's primary aim was to bundle, echo, and reframe residents' questions, so that Tijolero had to take them seriously. Tijolero's unguarded response, "That is right," when she reminded him that he had promised to vote in favor of "these questions" on the council provided leverage for the pro-CBA residents.

Without Anita's intervention, Tijolero would not have made such a revealing statement – a statement he would not repeal at the city hall meeting five days later.

Later, Anita explained to me that her team's disruptive strategy built on the work of social justice translators and aimed at deepening the levels of transparency and inclusivity in meetings:

> I learned a lot from Milana Fernandez, one of our SABAH translators, who is a student of simultaneous interpretation and who also teaches social justice translators and unionists in Florida. All of us have developed [this] ability very well.[14]

After Anita's intervention, meeting chair Maria took a stronger position, negotiating explicitly with Sal Tijolero, the council member, as a representative of her community. Tijolero avoided answering several questions she raised regarding his earlier promise to create a community park as part of the redevelopment project. Anita then intervened: "When exactly can we count on you [to get a park built]?" Tijolero: "It should take us between four to eight years." Anita reminded Tijolero of the need for legally binding principles to guarantee his promise of a park, and Tijolero answered simply: "The park is guaranteed." Anita began to ask increasingly specific questions, forcing him to be precise and accountable in his responses, and he seemed to try to evade her.

---

[14] My interview, Santa Brigida, June 18, 2010.

Although all participants spoke in Spanish, the dual presence of a community translator and a resident facilitator doubled the pressure on council member Tijolero. He found himself required to answer clearly and with great detail in the language all the residents understood, in contrast to his later failure to respond to residents at the June 7 city hall meeting.

THE LAST MINUTES: THREATS, CONFLICT, AND COMPROMISE

In the meeting's final minutes, tension mounted. Each time Anita intervened she received huge applause and chants: "CBA! CBA!" Faced with the crowd's discontent with his evasive tactics, Tijolero was forced to be more forthright. Growing more nervous, he finally voices an implicit threat against the SABAH coalition: "If you organize and put that much pressure on us, then in the end nothing will work out."

Maria: "We are only the community; we are not an organization."
Tijolero: "You are not an organization. You do not represent anyone but individuals. And that's why we can't sign an agreement with you. We only talk to organizations."
Maria repeated: "We are only the community."
Tijolero repeated: "We do not talk with the community. That is the law."
Maria: "We are the community. We want benefits."
Tijolero: "That is the law." [*Boos from the audience.*]
Maria's cofacilitator Ramon interrupted, calling forward the next council member: "Daniel, could you please come to the microphone?"

In this brief exchange with Tijolero, the two resident facilitators took different but complementary positions. In reaction to Anita's pointed questions, Tijolero used a threat against her organization, SABAH, and their mobilization of opposition to the project. But then Maria used her own leadership position as a resident to provide a counterargument ("We are only the community, not an organization"). To avoid more dialogue with Maria, Tijolero argued that politicians do not talk to individuals, implicitly questioning Maria's power as a voice on behalf of her community. At this point Maria's cofacilitator Ramon interrupted the stalemate to bring in another city council member, Daniel.

Daniel Bueno was the last council member to be questioned by the assembled residents. So far, neither of the other two council members at the meeting had made any concessions. Facilitator Maria proceeded to ask Bueno several pointed questions. After each one, the assembly applauded in support. From time to time, Anita assisted Maria by asking targeted questions aimed at disclosing Bueno's insider knowledge of the legal contracts surrounding the redevelopment project. Anita asked, "But why do you do you prefer a nonbinding contract to a Community Benefits Agreement?" Bueno answered: "Because it is a primary contract." A woman in the assembly raised her hand: "What is a primary contract?" Roberto, as translator and facilitator, took this question as an incentive to explain in Spanish that a CBA included a primary, binding contract that entailed the primary contractor, which was the developer, having full responsibility of implementing the project.

Roberto's translation clarified what Bueno's council members had previously omitted when they framed the CBA as either "too complicated" (Clark) or too difficult to implement because of legal issues (Tijolero). Council member Bueno's genuine answer to participants' critical questions revealed in fact that the city did not want to sign a CBA because the developing company did not wish to be constrained by the associated "primary contract," which would have assured that the community benefited effectively from the housing project as well.

Of all three city council members at the Community Forum, Bueno demonstrated the greatest openness and respect toward local residents. Unlike the two other professional politicians, he did not tell personal stories. Nor was his integrity contested. Nobody shouted at him as he concluded his comments. His presence had an immediate impact on the atmosphere in the assembly: participants who had angrily interrupted Tijolero listened attentively to Bueno. The "CBA" chants reemerged, but this time, notably fewer people joined in. Bueno did not try to justify his position, as the two before him had done. Unexpectedly, he announced that he and his colleagues at the final city hall meeting were going to support several changes proposed by residents in the discussion. Responding to questions left unanswered by the previous two council members, he explained in detail several proffered concessions, including how historical houses would be protected and who would benefit from the specific agreement proposed for the park. Silence followed Daniel Bueno's speech.

Roberto translated and thanked Bueno: "*Muchas gracias. OK, vamos.*" Roberto then announced that the assembly would vote on the development project on behalf of the community, but Maria interrupted him: "Not yet – we also have to hear what other council members have to say on these new agreements."

With these words, Maria strategically managed the adversarial setting and competition among the three present city council members. In the wake of Bueno's agreement to several of the residents' demands, she now asked the other two representatives for further concessions, including requests for a clear deadline for the building of a small park and a community center. Her strong position as negotiator stood in stark contrast to the shy, stuttering role she would take five days later as a participant in the city hall meeting.

Maria asked Sal Tijolero to come forward. He now affirmed his support for the points mentioned by Daniel, but still refused to endorse a CBA. He ended his statements by emphasizing the historical achievement of Latino/a city council members: "This is the first time in the history of the Marcy District that our people are benefiting from such a large state grant for urban redevelopment." A few people clapped. The local unionist sitting next to me commented quietly on Tijolero's self-promoting speech: "This is depressing."

Maria then asked her cofacilitator, Roberto, to come forward again. In Spanish, Roberto asked the assembly to take a final vote on behalf of the community: "If you are asked to choose, who among you would support a Community Benefits Agreement, a CBA, and who would like a Memorandum, or MoU?"

Virtually all of the people in the assembly raised their hands to support the legally binding CBA, and nobody raised a hand for the alternative nonbinding MoU proposed by city officials. After rousing applause, participants stood up, started chants, raised their CBA signs, and sang "Para el pueblo comunitario!" Before leaving the building, participants started doing *La Ola* (the wave), like fans at a sports arena: in the packed assembly, successive groups of participants briefly stood and raised their arms; then sat down again. The resulting wave of rising-and-falling bodies that traveled through the crowd symbolized the community's strength and solidarity.

AFTER THE VOTE: TRANSLATORS PUSH FOR POLICY CHANGE

The residents' collective vote had, formally at least, no direct impact on city government. Indeed, on June 7, the Santa Brigida City Council would vote against the CBA, which residents at this meeting supported unanimously. However, despite the council's continuing disagreement with SABAH coalition leaders, the unusual style of deliberation and negotiation at the Community Forum provoked an important compromise. City council member Bueno told me later:

A lot of issues ended up being integrated in our [*the city council's*] decision as a result of that conversation [*in the Community Forum*]: first, regarding the community center; second, the park; third, money set apart for future investments; forth, a recreation area for retail; fifth, a small community store; and sixth, several opportunities of affordable housing – over a hundred. Many of those items were in direct response to concerns raised by community members. SABAH wanted a legal contract with their group; we [*the city council*] decided to enter their proposals but not enter into a legal contract. The vote at the end of the meeting [*the forum*] meant to me that we integrated what they wanted.[15]

When Bueno said that the city council had "integrated" what the community "wanted," he was distinguishing "they" – the community as a whole – from the SABAH coalition leadership, whom the council distrusted and who was behind the CBA demand. The critical organizing work by Anita and others at the Community Forum seemed not to register with him or the other city council members.

By my count, Anita and other SABAH community translators interrupted politicians twenty times during the two hours of the community-based meeting. For this reason, I was surprised that the city council members did not recognize the translators' implicit political negotiation work in helping residents get concessions. When I later interviewed Bueno about his relationship to the translators, he said:

[15] My interview, Santa Brigida, June 19, 2010.

We council members understand people, I think we get there. Intent is just the way we change things. I get energized by being able to hear from people; that's our job, I appreciate that. It's important for people to have an audience, fill a room, be heard. At the same time, what was intimidating, there was a lot of passion. You want to hear but also say something. We want to make decisions and sometimes there will be different opinions, a deal, or also you want to ask questions yourself. They timed us for [only] one minute for each question.[16]

Daniel Bueno's statement suggests that he did not comprehend the full impact of the translators' interventions, which apparently did not bother the politicians. He perceived the time limits imposed on city council members as constraining, but also admitted being "energized" by the meeting. He saw Anita and other community organizers as useful linguistic translators, without noticing the subtle ways in which they extended the accredited role of a linguistic translator through their interventions. Yet through their interventions and the timing of the agenda, the community translators had prevented the professional politicians from systematically interrupting other participants as they would at the city hall meeting on June 7. From the residents' perspective, therefore, the presence of community translators had greatly improved the conditions for passionate and egalitarian debate between the otherwise unequal groups of professional politicians and disadvantaged residents.

From the perspective of local community organizers like Anita, the compromise reached at the SABAH forum was not sufficient, because city hall continued to refuse to agree to a CBA. SABAH community translators therefore continued to organize Community Forum meetings to press this point and to follow up on the councilors to check whether the promises that had been agreed upon were actually being implemented in ongoing policy-making.

Although they had not succeeded in changing any of the councilors' minds about the CBA, they had gotten one of the councilors, Daniel, to make explicit commitments on which they could follow up. And they had impressed all three council members with the community's power.

In addition to energizing the community, extracting specific concessions, and impressing all three council members with the fierce dedication of the residents who attended the meetings, Anita and her group of community translators seemed also to have had an effect on the thinking of at least one member of the council. When Bueno described his participation at the forum to me, he even seemed to have borrowed some of his vocabulary from Anita and other SABAH members, including the idea of being "intentional" about building relationships to the community, a term that Anita had made council members familiar with.[17]

Before and after each of the forum meetings, SABAH community translators had visited Bueno and other city council members in their offices, where they reminded them of the importance of building dialogue with residents through

[16] My interview, Santa Brigida, June 19, 2010.
[17] Daniel: "Intent is just the way we change things."

ongoing community meetings. The SABAH coalition divided its work strategically. While some members focused on interventions during meetings, others focused on outreach, including building and maintaining close, trusting relationships with politicians. The existence of this strategic, dialogue-oriented outreach to the politicians made possible the critical and disruptive visible public interventions at the forum by SABAH community translators. Anita and her colleagues were able to act as officially accredited community translators precisely because their visible work at the forums was reinforced by their behind-the-scenes meetings with the city council members. This combination of dialogue and disruption, intimate connection to and distance from dominant leaders is characteristic of much collective work of grassroots political translators, in both adversarial and more common-interested situations such as those in the Social Forums.

DISCUSSION: THE ART OF POLITICAL TRANSLATION IN ADVERSARIAL DEMOCRACY

Following standard accounts in democratic theory, one would assume that local democracy works inclusively if disadvantaged groups can elect their own representatives. The events in Santa Brigida, however, suggest that elected representation is not enough. Despite their earlier career in progressive NGOs and community projects and their progressive intentions, all three council members voted in favor of a housing project profiting commercial interests rather than addressing residents' urgent demands to safeguard future opportunities for affordable housing in the Marcy neighborhood. This kind of conflict of interest, all too common when elected officials lose their primary identification with those they purportedly represent, makes representative democracy ineffective.

The grassroots community translators, working as independent third parties, were able to act as a collectively as a critical force for building political dialogue in which residents could effectively represent their own interests. While active deliberation was blocked in the antagonistic office setting of city hall, an unusually passionate form of deliberation emerged at the SABAH Community Forum, thanks to the informal power of the grassroots community translators.

Samantha Clark, Sal Tijolero, and Daniel Bueno all considered themselves dedicated representatives of the first- and second-generation immigrant community in Santa Brigida. They had been duly elected to office through free and fair elections in that community. They attended community meetings and held office hours open to all members of the community. But their strong presence in the city hall meeting was not enough to make the members of that community feel at home. They all – including Daniel Bueno, the most sensitive to community sentiment – seemed to miss the subtle interactions that foregrounded residents at the forum but marginalized them at city hall.

Anita and the SABAH team of community translators had crafted the alternative SABAH Community Forum to bring out the voices of the residents. They controlled the timing and scheduling of speakers, the subjects debated, and the knowledge shared. They ensured that professional politicians did not silence any resident speaker. The setting they created was coercive because it shaped the channels through which people spoke. For example, it forced professional politicians to answer their constituents directly and specifically. In this forum, first, one of city council members and then the others changed their blockade position toward residents' questions and were persuaded to agree to demands for clarification and concessions. As translators of more than language, Anita and her team provided transparent insights into the city's planned actions, making it possible to hold policy-makers accountable for their decisions. Several of the residents turned into expert translators who were able to decrypt for others the institutional language of development and administrative law.

The grassroots political translation in Santa Brigida's SABAH Community Forum was a multifaceted task shared by paid community organizers and resident immigrants. The Community Forum enabled monolingual Spanish-speaking working class residents to speak confidently, chair the meeting themselves, and eventually persuade reluctant city council members to answer important questions and agree to several valuable concessions.

Democratic theorists have started to explore the overlap and connections between representative democracy (based on elections) and radical/participatory democracy. As illustrated by the SABAH forum, political translators' interventions and presence encouraged previously unrepresented groups to speak for themselves as a collective and push forward their arguments in public deliberation.

What distinguishes the political translators in Santa Brigida from those in the European Social Forum and Atlanta was that they included local residents directly affected by policy-making, many of them immigrants. At the SABAH Community Forum, the community-organizer translators and the resident facilitators acted as a team and shaped the entire course of the negotiation. Anita and her SABAH team did not claim to speak on behalf of resident immigrants. Instead, as second-generation immigrants, they connected their own struggle for empowerment and education with the struggles of local resident immigrants, such as Maria and Roberto. Anita herself believes that democracy depends on changing relationships, as well as shifting relational and social boundaries, through deliberate dialogue. She told me that she and Maria had become *compañeras* through the co-decision-making practices in the SABAH coalition. "I sometimes take care of Maria's grandchildren," she said. As *compañeras*, the residents and community translators take different, complementary positions supporting each other, as when in the contentious last minutes at the SABAH forum, Maria intervened to protect Anita and her organization by invoking her own dual position as resident and forum leader.

The most surprising finding in Santa Brigida was that the visible interventions by SABAH community translators during councilors' negotiations with the residents were not recognized as a political practice, and thus not perceived as a threat, by established city council members. Yet almost all the city council members saw political activism in general and the leaders of the SABAH coalitions in particular as threats to their power positions at city hall. Santa Brigida's city hall meetings were riddled with formal and informal inequities, of which city council members seemed completely ignorant. Because they were not aware of the destructive and marginalizing dynamics of the positional misunderstandings in which they had been involved at the city hall meetings, the city council members were not aware of the communicative power of the SABAH community translators at the forum.

The case of Santa Brigida indicates that when deliberation can be assisted by a group of grassroots political translators, those in power may begin to respond to positional misunderstandings, of which they are often unaware.

CONCLUSION

A New Model for Deliberation

Over the past two decades, thousands of global justice activists in Europe and the United States have practiced political translation at the World Social Forum (WSF) – the largest face-to-face democracy experiment anywhere. Coming from a variety of national backgrounds and ideologies, these activists have made it possible for the European Social Forum (ESF) and the United States Social Forum (USSF) to bring large numbers of additional citizens, immigrants, and speakers of multiple languages into deliberation about social justice and financial, economic, and environmental politics.

Drawing on eight years of fieldwork involving case studies of forty Social Forum meetings and local citizen forums, I have shown how political translators helped citizens with a variety of linguistic and national affiliations to work together effectively – and *more* democratically than citizens in monolingual, culturally homogeneous civic groups. Previous studies of deliberative and participatory democracy would probably have predicted the opposite, assuming that multiple languages would obstruct the work of the group. Yet I found strong evidence that whenever multilingual and culturally diverse situations involved collective interventions by groups of grassroots political translators, they were more inclusive, democratic, and effective than homogeneous settings.

In my four case studies, political translators intervened collectively – that is, from a loose, informal, and ephemeral organizational base – to address the systematic failure of democratic deliberation to include disadvantaged groups. A political translation collective begins when informal groups of cultural or linguistic translators organize themselves after witnessing the marginalizing of some forum participants. Much of political translation begins with linguistic translation, whose intermediary role of the "third" it resembles, although political translation departs from the conventional role understandings of linguistic interpretation. As in the case of the Babels at the ESF, political translation collectives are often headed by cultural or linguistic intermediaries who are acutely aware of inequality and marginalization in the context of political deliberation in diverse and asymmetric social contexts.

Political translation builds on two interrelated mechanisms of consciousness-raising and advocacy. First and most importantly, recognizing linguistic differences and linguistic marginalization can lead to discussion of other forms of marginalization and possibilities for accommodation. When members of a group speak different languages, the differences within the group are easily perceptible; they also come with a built-in justification for remediation. If one language dominates the proceedings, everyone agrees that those who do not speak that language must labor under a disadvantage. The need to address linguistic inequalities then sets the stage for opening conceptual, emotional, and organizational paths to understanding and redressing other forms of marginalization and conflict within the group – among them class and gender inequalities, which also often distort communication.

The second mechanism, following from the first, entails explicit advocacy for those who have not been fully "heard." In the ESF, voluntary linguistic translators gradually developed a practice of advocating explicitly for the deliberative equality of the groups they served – including groups marginalized not only by dint of language or nationality but, in some cases, by gender or social class. This advocacy turned the volunteers into political translators. Because in the Social Forums the translators' status approached that of the facilitators, they were able to intervene authoritatively. In other groups, such as the US Social Forum, where linguistic translation was not always necessary, the position of the political translators merged with that of cultural intermediaries who had somewhat central positions in the informal power structure and collectively started to advocate specifically for identified marginalized groups.

For democratic theorists, political translation provides a new way of conceptualizing the dynamics of inequality as sources of internal conflict, stalemate, or democratic crisis in deliberative politics and public participation. Even in organizations devoted to social change, conscious action is required to create equal access to power and influence when some group(s) subtly or openly possess greater power. A third party explicitly tasked with redressing imbalances in access can be very effective in this role.

In institutionalized participatory democracy, the standard model of formally neutral, egalitarian facilitation is prone to conscious and unconscious manipulation. In the case of Santa Brigida's participatory city hall meetings, facilitation was carried out by institutional insiders, including high-ranking city council officials and politicians. The facilitators' formal neutrality served as a gate-keeping instrument that allowed dominant groups to push their preferred decisions through, even as the facilitator restricted the expressions and arguments of residents by controlling the setting of agendas, the selection of speakers, and the timing and order of presentations by staffers and elected representatives.

In the cases I studied, even self-consciously egalitarian facilitation in the Social Forums failed to involve all groups on an equal basis; the facilitators in these situations proved unable to remain truly impartial, which would have required including the voices of disadvantaged groups even when their interests conflicted with those of the dominant groups. The Social Forums, based on the principles of consensus based, or deliberative democracy, broke apart even when benevolent facilitators had been trained with feminist consensus methods and tried their best to be inclusive: they still found themselves unable to stop small, disproportionately powerful factions from disproportionately influencing decisions.

While the patterns of domination varied across the cases and contexts studied, it was generally the case that materially privileged groups and individuals tended to take over deliberative processes. In several of the cases, consensus processes failed to be inclusive because the self-consciously egalitarian facilitators were inadvertently unable to separate their own interests from those of dominant groups. I think it's fair to say that "neutral" facilitation is impossible – and this raises the urgent question of how to counterbalance the inevitable personal and cultural biases of individual facilitators.

The practice of political translation shows that these problems are not insurmountable. Translators experienced with linguistic and cultural heterogeneity have demonstrated the strategic insight and the political capacity necessary to induce institutional insiders and elites, often including facilitators themselves, to respond to marginalized populations. I see political translation as one example of the larger possibility of a third force intervening in deliberative dynamics to help level the playing field between well-meaning yet sometimes insensitive dominant groups and groups marginalized in the deliberative process.

The cases in this study illuminate the problems of inequality and marginalization even within social movements committed to equality, like those cooperating in the WSF process. In core political conflicts about resource inequality in the regional ESF and the USSF coalition, political deliberation turned from a justice-oriented empathetic process of mutual listening into a struggle for power among participating groups and individuals. Like the "vibes watchers" in previous social movement coalitions (Taylor 1995), political translators were able to intervene to create awareness of the process of marginalization within the deliberative arenas.

POSITIONAL MISUNDERSTANDINGS AND INEQUALITY

Political translators transcend the ideals of neutrality and impartiality in response to what I have called *positional misunderstandings* – impasses that arise when dominant groups deliberately or inadvertently disregard disadvantaged groups' political arguments. At the core of positional misunderstandings usually lie differences of material interest or ideology, which often materialize during public debate when more powerful groups dismiss arguments made by the less powerful, characterizing them as making no sense. In Santa Brigida, progressive city councilors passionately declared their inability to understand residents' concerns about a controversial redevelopment proposal that threatened many with eviction. One city councilman exclaimed to the residents that instead of protesting against the city government, they should "celebrate with us." Another added: "I don't understand you [residents]! You don't get the complexity. You simply don't get it."[1] Council members were right: government decision-making even at the local level does involve a high level of complexity and frequently painful trade-offs for elected representatives – challenges of which ordinary citizens are not always aware. Yet positional misunderstandings often involve a strong element of denial on the part of the dominant group, which may refuse to acknowledge either the urgency of the situation or the necessity of rethinking the consequences of their decisions. Positional misunderstandings thus signal a conscious or unconscious unwillingness on the part of the privileged to surrender to the legitimacy of arguments made by less privileged groups. Although positional misunderstandings can work on both sides, their political impact is usually asymmetric. To take an example not explored in this book, in an ESF preparatory assembly in Istanbul in 2005, a dominant group of Western European ESF elites found themselves in a stalemated a debate with resource-poor grassroots activists from Turkey. Western European ESF insiders, many of whom had been engaged for years in exchanges with activists from Turkey, wanted the local activists from Istanbul to join the upcoming large-scale ESF event scheduled to take place in Athens in 2006. The facilitator in the Istanbul meeting, who came from Western Europe, used the phrase "The Europeans have decided ..." to strengthen her proposal for the final consensus on the political theme of the planned ESF event.[2] After her speech, however, dozens of local activists stood up to denounce that consensus proposal, which ignored both their discussion contributions and their wish as newcomers take part in joint decision-making regarding the upcoming ESF event. It was only after the team of political translators intervened that the facilitator began to realize that her thoughtless use of the phrasing "the Europeans have decided" had reignited in local participants a strong sense of marginalization based on Eurocentrism. This one instance typifies of hundreds of interventions by political translators who helped activists work together across cultural divides and power asymmetries characterizing the European assemblies of the ESF.

Positional misunderstandings thus arise from something more than simple incomprehension. Privileged parties in deliberation, particularly in democratic social movements, often express publicly that they "understand" other groups and feel empathy for the less privileged. But positional misunderstandings are clashes of normative values and material interests. While in principle a relatively privileged group may wish benevolently to engage in open and direct dialogue with another, less privileged group, the effort may still end in conflict

---

[1] My fieldnotes.   [2] My fieldnotes.

and disagreement. Those with privilege are typically unable to take to heart a dissenting point of view that might challenge their agenda, while the less privileged claim – sometimes misconstruing the intent – that they have been willfully ignored.

Although neglected in previous research, positional misunderstandings lie at the core of much of the injustice, inequality, and systematic marginalization that occur within, and are legitimated through, participatory, deliberative, and consensus-oriented democratic processes.

In all four national Social Forum cases in this study, once finances were at issue, social movement elites, NGOs, and institutional funders found ways to sideline the arguments made by less privileged groups, despite the shared goal of consensus-based decision-making. Progressive philanthropic foundations and NGOs withdrew their funding from the USSF coalition, for example, when grassroots activists asked them to share national leadership positions more equally with minorities and immigrants. So too in the national preparatory meetings of the ESF, powerful unionists and institutional leftist party organizers in Italy, the United Kingdom, and Germany refused to share the available political resources with noninstitutionalized groups.

In the national social movement meetings in Europe that took place without political translators, these positional misunderstandings had immediate consequences, signaling the impending end of democratic cooperation across insider-outsider lines. Feeling misunderstood and marginalized during deliberations, immigrants, precarious workers, LGBT, and anarchist groups were among the first to quit the deliberative process in the national Social Forums, often followed by others who chose to exit after dramatic protests in meetings spread the feeling of injustice among participants.

While the marginalized often enter the deliberations with little trust in the privileged and soon find their mistrust confirmed, the privileged often remain utterly unaware of their own entangled role. Even leaders directly involved in marginalizing other groups may suffer a continuing lack of awareness about what has caused stalemate and divided the movement. Several years after the German Social Forum (GSF) had collapsed, one of the GSF facilitators whom many had blamed personally for the biased consensus practices told me earnestly that he was still trying to figure out what exactly had gone wrong. "If only I knew," he said in the interview, "if only I could understand why we have never been able to become friends."[3] Positional misunderstandings then beget feelings of mutual frustration and pain as well as the loss of a beneficial cooperative relationship between groups.

In the position of witnessing, disruptive third party, political translators have the power to intervene in such impasses. Because the volunteer translators' role in multilingual settings like the Santa Brigida community meetings or the

[3] My interview, January 30, 2010, and my translation from the original German.

European assemblies of the ESF was to ensure *mutuality* in conversation, translators could not help noticing the unwillingness of privileged groups to attend seriously to legitimate arguments made by less privileged groups. As witnesses of stalemate, they were also aware that the privileged persistently tend to argue in public that the only possible option is what they themselves want.

Translators become *political* translators by disrupting their own cooperative relationships with dominant groups and taking a moral stand, explaining that they can no longer remain silent in the face of injustice and marginalization. Temporarily interrupting their essential work without relinquishing their moral commitment to ongoing dialogue, they symbolically demonstrate that even the privileged depend upon others. In so doing, they may increase privileged groups' understanding of arguments made by less privileged groups. As they interrupt the implicit relationship of domination that causes positional misunderstandings, they support the deliberative project.

POLITICAL TRANSLATION, TRANSNATIONAL ARENAS, AND DEMOCRACY IN DIVERSE SOCIETIES

My central argument is that truly democratic dialogue in diverse groups and structurally unequal societies depends on institutionalizing a third position for political translation. The collectives of political translators that I saw emerge independently in Europe and the United States used political translation as a foundational model for democracy, in the process developing an oppositional consciousness.

Political translation allows for the perception of difference as a resource for democracy in increasingly multilingual, globalized societies. While previous political theorists have conceptualized democracy as closely tied to the nation-state, these studies indicate that the Social Forum experiments in democracy were more inclusive and transparent at the transnational level than at the national level; inclusive, effective decision-making was more easily reached through political translation in contexts with the greatest cultural diversity, that is, within the transnational, multilingual Social Forums. At the national level, when activists addressed intersecting cultural differences and conflicts about race using political translation, their USSF coalition succeeded in overcoming deep internal conflicts – in contrast with the collapse of national Social Forums like the GSF, which without internal political translations failed to address these questions. Because political translators address cultural marginalization *and* structural inequality, their practices have the capacity to instill in all deliberators a commitment to engage not only linguistic differences but also differences of identity and ideology.

Students of cosmopolitan and multicultural democracy and political activists in multilingual societies can conclude from these cases that political translation can dramatically improve the inclusivity and effectiveness of decision-making practices in diverse movement groups and local democratic settings. Most importantly, one language is not necessarily better than two. Although most well-known models of deliberative democracy assume a single, universalist language model, in my cases such models were not effective at including all participants in the shared discourse – and instead, marginalized, for example, women and minorities. As a solution to the many-language problem, cosmopolitan thinkers promote the idea of a global lingua franca, while multiculturalists prefer to utilize the vernacular languages. As I have shown, political translation can be effective in both kinds of setting. In both the national context of the USSF and the transnational arena of the ESF, it trained participants in a new way of cooperating with groups from different backgrounds, bridging boundaries of race, nationality, class, and gender. The trusting relationships that translators fostered in the ESF, for example, demonstrate the power of deliberative rituals that facilitate shared experiences in arenas characterized by difference (Polletta 2002). The potential for cosmopolitan deliberation in multilingual arenas is thus not confined to closed institutional settings among global elites (Lamont and Aksartova 2002).

From a comparative perspective, the emerging practices of political translation illustrate how transnational social movements can transform previously nationally and domestically oriented public spaces. Although the creation of the nation-state and national media systems have contributed to the institutionalization of a single national language in many countries, translation is now becoming a medium for communication across countries and groups, from social movements to institutional actors. More recently, Social Forum actors have begun to adopt the practice of political translation in order to increase the power of social movements in negotiations involving institutional actors, such as the European Parliament and the European Trade Union Federation (Doerr 2012). The cases presented here suggest that political translation may be critical for democracy in diverse societies and multilingual political institutions.

CULTURE, UNACKNOWLEDGED GROUP DIFFERENCES, AND THE DISRUPTIVE THIRD

The most surprising finding to emerge from these cases is perhaps that the visible and disruptive interventions by political translators in deliberations involving politicians or informal social movement elites were not recognized as a political practice, and thus not perceived as a threat by the groups and individuals dominating the deliberative process. This nonthreatening quality of the interaction appeared even in the contentious context of local urban politics in the United States, where in the town of Santa Brigida, California, almost all the city council members saw any political activism as a threat to their own power positions at city hall (Chapter 3).

The reason why political translators' influence remained partly unacknowledged and so could pass the power-radar of politicians and dominant groups lies in the nature of positional misunderstandings. Throughout this book I have revealed the preconscious nature of miscommunications between dominant groups and others, which has been addressed by previous work. Sociologists have explored the precognitive nature of misunderstandings in political parti-cipation based on different embodied local habits of organizing that may create cultural "clashes" even between different groups sharing a political ideology (Flesher Fominaya 2015). Differences in "group style" (Eliasoph and Lichterman 2003) or class cultural differences impede building more diverse, intersectional social movement coalitions (Leondar-Wright 2014). Within poli-tical deliberation, dominant *habits of hearing* restrict the impact of valid points made by disadvantaged groups and individuals (Polletta 2006; Doerr 2011). By getting at the preconscious dynamics of misunderstandings in groups, we can understand how dominant styles, habits, or practices get recreated within ostensibly inclusive participation or deliberation. The dominant habits revealed in the cases in this book were typically those of professional politicians or groups such as the facilitators, who perceived their own culturally distinct style as "neutral" and "universal" (Young 1996; Smith 2017).

Activists and community organizers in different places have used the prac-tice of political translation in order to foster a self-reflective learning process and change of embodied dominant habits. The practice combines disruption and persuasion to broaden the spectrum of what can be seen and heard and said in coalitions among all members. It is a micropractice to illustrate how social change can occur at the cognitive and emotional level in communicative encounters across difference. Political translation as a concept helps reveal what activists and practitioners can do to avoid undue domination by one particular way of doing things.

When the Western Europeans ignored this disagreement with their local grassroots allies and proceeded to push forward a final decision on the political theme for the planned Athens ESF event, the "Babels" political translators intervened a second time. As in Paris, the Babels stopped translat-ing in order to signal to the dominant ESF elites that they needed to treat local activists with greater respect. The ESF elites listened and apologized to locals, so that a true dialogue between Western Europeans and local Turkish and Kurdish grassroots activists could commence. The political translators' inter-ruption not only broke the stalemate, it also improved the position of local participants' interests in the final consensus agreement.

Istanbul, like Paris and the other cases in this book, demonstrates that while not directly taking sides, political translators can collectively intervene as an independent third force within deliberation and demonstrate to domi-nant group members that there is a mutually beneficial alternative way of interacting with other group members, a way that the dominant members have often been unwilling to acknowledge on their own.

Political translation is a new way to connect theories of protest and deliberative democratic politics. Previous theorists of deliberation have separated protest and political contention from dialogue and deliberative politics. They have argued that the expression of open protest, emotion, and political disruption would endanger the culture of rational, detached discussion on which deliberation is built (see, critically, Polletta 2006, 2015). Previous work has also conceptualized activists as either contentious political actors who engage strategically and instrumentally within discursive arenas, or as deliberative advocates arguing on behalf of the common good (see critically, Bob 2005; Risse 2000). But at the heart of political translation is the combination of disruption and persuasion. Political translators disrupt the deliberative process when it is unfair while persuading and teaching institutional elites how to democratize deliberation. Although many scholars have studied the marginalization that occurs within supposedly inclusive deliberative settings, few have written about the implications of opposition being silenced within consensus-based democratic forms (Deitelhoff and Thiel 2014). Political translation is a way of including opposition within deliberative democratic arenas.

Political translation provides a model for activists to intervene in stalemate situations to realize what Arendt calls "power with," or the collective power of a deliberative assembly to foster decisions for the common good (Arendt 1958; Habermas 1977). Deliberative democracy builds on the power of strong arguments to convince well-intentioned dominant groups to come to beneficial agreements. Political translation reaches beyond the deliberative ideal of rational argument and persuasion to access collective power; it is not fully coercive but rather uses collective pressure based on the principles of nonviolent resistance and principled action (Chabot and Vintagen 2007; Vintagen 2015). In the situations I observed, political translators induced dominant groups to listen to and be convinced by voices that they had previously been unwilling to recognize as equals within their previous political deliberations. Such breakdowns of empathy through positional misunderstandings occur, for example, during crisis situations in political deliberation when dominant groups feel the need to make a "tough" and timely decision, as politicians in Santa Brigida affirmed, or to "get things done," as NGOs and institutionalized Social Forum supporters in the United States and in Europe phrased it.

I do not propose to replace the position of facilitator with that of political translator. Rather, I propose to reconceptualize democracy by considering that in situations of asymmetric power, a third, independent force needs to monitor and balance the influence of dominant groups, including that of purportedly neutral facilitators when they disproportionately represent the interests of privileged groups. Political translation promotes egalitarianism; it also channels protest toward constructive ends. Where neutral facilitators are usually concerned with taming protest and emotion in deliberation, political translation can facilitate constructive expression of protests, emotions, and even chants, allowing the assembly to build a collective force that the powerful can no longer ignore, and ultimately helping draw out underlying concrete arguments that can influence decision-making.

DEMOCRACY, COALITION BUILDING, AND LEADERSHIP IN DIVERSE SOCIAL MOVEMENTS

It is often hard for progressive transnational coalitions to achieve democratic agreements and to avoid domination by resource-rich groups, which tend to be based in the global North. The transnational ESF survived for almost ten years with grassroots political translators intervening to prevent several internal democratic crises arising from related power asymmetries. Without such interventions, all the parallel national Social Forum processes I studied collapsed.

Political translation also provides a new model for social movement leadership in the context of intersectional coalitions. In both the USSF in Atlanta and the SABAH coalition in Santa Brigida, California, political translators found or built grassroots activist and immigrant leadership to intervene in key debates about finance policy, even against the opposition of the philanthropic foundations in Atlanta and the city councilors in Santa Brigida.

When the founders of the USSF witnessed the absence of a whole new generation of local leaders from among immigrants, people-of-color, and LGBT movements, they developed a new variety of intersectional translating practices required in heterogeneous coalitions (Robnett 1997; Roth 2003; Smith 2005; Wood 2005). Political translators are not just minority advocates; nor are they strategic brokers. Like advocates, they promote the good of the disadvantaged. Like strategic brokers, they occupy an intermediary position between different groups. Unlike advocates or brokers, the leverage of political translators is based on their cultural and linguistic capacity to recognize positional misunderstandings. Beyond instrumentalist notions of advocacy or of brokerage, political translators see themselves as grassroots educators who address the inequalities that create stalemates within intramovement deliberation and decision-making. Political translators do not actively mediate or broker consensus decisions; they intervene to interrupt unfair decision-making and educate dominant elites about cultural bias and inequality.

The idea of political translation challenges the culturally neutral idea of "horizontal" network leadership in the consensus-based democracy of the global justice movement. Even within these highly egalitarian movements, institutional social movement elites naturally take the positions of conflict mediators and facilitators. Thinking of themselves as network brokers, mediators, or neutral facilitators, these elites often promote the interests of the most influential groups within their coalitions, while alienating or actively marginalizing other participants. This model is flawed. In my experience, only some other version of a disruptive third, like political translation, can counter-balance the informal power of NGO staffers, market-based funders, and institutional leftist organizers within movement coalitions.

To accomplish its goals, political translation must be temporary. Otherwise, political translators could become a new political force and introduce a new dominant leadership style.

In Atlanta, for example, the political translators of the USSF used their professional experiences as intersectional grassroots educators to increase the power of minority groups, including mainly low-income community members, blacks, Latinos, immigrants, LGBT activists, and indigenous groups. For a while, the USSF political translators increased their own leverage as a necessary cultural intermediary. Yet within the negotiations at the national planning assembly, the political translators' power vanished, as the newly empowered groups imposed their preferences in the decision-making process. The political translators helped others to take a bigger role within national political deliberation. The individuals who had initiated political translation at the USSF then moved on to other, newly emerging democratic processes. Political translators can avoid the trap of political power as long as they focus their energies on a commitment to democratic practice and plan to remove themselves or divert their energies elsewhere.

It is also essential that those assigned the responsibilities of political translation not hold positions of structural power in relation to the deliberations they serve. In Santa Brigida, the elected representatives claimed to speak in the name of their constituencies, while at the same time consciously and unconsciously silencing constituents' voices in public deliberation. This case strongly suggests that members of dominant groups – even ostensibly representative elected actors who sincerely have the interests of the disadvantaged in mind – cannot act as political translators. Political translation can only be carried out by members of independent groups whose position is one of political marginality within the decision-making.

VARYING POLITICAL TRANSLATION STRATEGIES
IN DIFFERENT CONTEXTS

Political translation practices must vary depending on the context and on the translators' experience, knowledge, strategy, and leverage. Social structures and organizational patterns can constrain the prospects for political translation. In Santa Brigida, the officially supplied physical space for political deliberation was so constraining that grassroots political translators did not disrupt the official arena but instead constructed an alternative public space, the SABAH community forum, for their democratic interventions. In a more open social movement forum like the ESF, political translators intervened directly, seeking to transform some of the mainstream norms and practices of consensus dominated by unionists and leftist political party elites.

Although I found no evidence of direct diffusion among the three political translation collectives studied, their emancipatory practices evolved from the same premise: a need to address inequality and cultural diversity within deliberative or participatory democratic settings. The intellectual history of the groups' political translation practices varied across the different cases and contexts. For example, the Atlanta team applied political translation as a grassroots leadership model for transcending and transforming the racial, gendered, and spatial power hierarchies within their coalition, drawing on the diverse experiences of immigrants and language justice educators, disability rights, LGBT, feminist, and people-of-color organizers, and Native American leaders. Both the Atlanta political translation team and the community translators in Santa Brigida included several activists trained in language justice interpretation, a practice which is broadly used by immigrants'-rights and civil-rights organizers across the United States and trained at Highlander Research and Education Center in Tennessee (Tijerina 2009). In comparison, the Babels at the ESF based their disruptive interventions as political translators on their normative belief in the Social Forum as an inclusive, "horizontal," and transparent deliberative space (Boéri and Hodkinson 2004). The Babels' linguistic practices as volunteer translators focused on building an inclusive multilingual meeting was also based on their founders' professional skills as simultaneous interpreters (Boéri 2010).

Founders' influence and preference for a particular ideology of political translation may in fact limit and constrain the diffusion or extension of emerging translating practices to other fields or contexts (Blee 2012). For example, several of the Babels founders were trained and experienced in simultaneous interpretation; their political activism aimed at applying this professional background to their activism (Boéri 2010). Their network's focus on the translation of linguistic differences might have precluded extending their style of political translation to monolingual contexts like the national Social Forum groups. In comparison, the relatively diverse founding group of the Atlanta political translators' collective included LGBT and gender justice organizers as well as immigrants and bilingual language justice translators; their combined knowledge and insights enabled them to extend their efforts beyond language justice translation to helping bridge differences of race and gender as well. Providing a local example for this, community translators and residents in Santa Brigida traced their self-consciously disruptive translation style back to the "contamination" and mutual inspiration with different experiences of language justice interpreting and grassroots education (della Porta and Mosca 2007). They combined grassroots education, Latino empowerment, and their personal experiences as first- and second-generation immigrants working in bilingual local environments, with English being the dominant official language and Spanish the language of working-class people and resident immigrants.

Political translators' leverage also depends on the linguistic and cultural context, and particularly on how organizers define the need for political translation. A favorable context would be, for example, a public discussion or coalition setting with visible cultural or linguistic differences, or a level of inequality high enough to justify working with a group of cultural intermediaries. In monolingual settings, some individuals may be designated as cultural intermediaries, who may transform into a collective of political translators during moments of crisis in the political dialogue. Sometimes the content may demand significant disruption, as in Paris, at the ESF, where political translators used the disruptive strategy of striking to make the ESF political elites aware of the marginalizing effects of their actions. Here the translators had the power to block the consensus process: the negotiation could not proceed without them. While this openly contentious practice worked in the specific context of the ESF in Paris, it might not have succeeded in other cultural and political contexts.

In the USSF in Atlanta, for example, political translators avoided contentious interventions during meetings and used their implicit leverage as trustworthy cultural intermediaries, known by funders and institutional NGOs, to increase the presence of minorities and immigrants in national meetings. Only by combining pressure and continuous interventions vis-à-vis funders could these founders and political translators slowly increase awareness among institutional elites of the need to include arguments made by previously unheard local groups and people of color. Their informal strategy of political translation made it much harder for those who had funded the Social Forum to continue avoiding issues of race, class, and gender in debates, and it encouraged a perceived extraordinary level of mutual learning and connection across cultural boundaries.

In all cases, political translation collectives depend in a complex way both on the strategic interest of dominant groups to cooperate and create a dialogue with disadvantaged communities and on the translators' collective willingness and ability to resist attempts by the dominant elites to communicate in just one direction.

CONDITIONS OF APPLICABILITY

Political translation is relevant in every asymmetrical public discussion setting that gains legitimacy based on a dialogue-oriented or deliberative model. But it can succeed only when certain conditions are in place.

First, the social and political elites in the community must, at a minimum, be interested in entering into dialogue with disadvantaged groups on the attempted footing of political equality. To some degree, political translation can have an impact even if dominant elites do not initially want to listen to disadvantaged groups. Political translators or other organizers can sometimes use persuasion to get elites to the table but then take up contentious action and protest within the public space they had created. In Santa Brigida, for example, political translators started with strategic outreach to dominant elites; they built individual trust with several relatively progressive politicians then used their accreditation to perform disruptive interventions aimed at the same politicians during deliberation, and they followed up to make sure elites implemented the actual changes they had agreed to.

Second, the elites must see a need for a collective intermediary. This may mean that cultural heterogeneity is indirectly a condition for a political translation collective to emerge. Linguistic differences give elites an obvious reason to work with translators. Because the politicians in Santa Brigida spoke the same language as their constituents, they assumed they did not need to work with a translator. A key early task of political translators is to convince dominant elites that it is a good idea to work with intermediaries in order to address cultural diversity and social inequality within a deliberative process. The perceived divides need not always stem from linguistic difference. In Atlanta, issues of race allowed USSF founders to claim the role of political translators for themselves, while absence of a race cleavage impeded the emergence of a political translation collective in the culturally more homogeneous context of the GSF in Frankfurt.

Third, an intermediary party must be available to take a position between dominant and dominated groups. This third position is key in the political translators' leverage of dominated groups and their empathetic connection with disadvantaged groups. The translator has the difficult task of constantly maintaining dialogue in these two directions, of "holding" a political space that balances and maintains an egalitarian relationship across the differences. To maintain this intermediate position, political translators require a certain level of financial and organizational independence from dominant insiders, and they also need a collective motivation and an oppositional consciousness in order to take the risk of disrupting positional misunderstandings – even when neutral facilitators or group elites try to quell those disruptions.

They also need to develop the patience, and the intercultural knowledge to communicate across perspectives and to empathize with the perspective of dominant groups without giving in to their pressure, financial or otherwise. They need some minimum level of leverage in relation to the dominant group in order to be recognized as legitimate brokers during the conflict situation; otherwise they will be ignored. The translators' heterogeneous backgrounds and skills will help a team of political translators to complement each other's work.

Fourth and finally, no single political translator can act on her own; she needs to be part of a team. In the many instances I observed, none of the participants who stood up individually within an assembly and attempted to intervene as a political translator for another participant was successful. When individual immigrants'-

rights activists, feminists, or anarchists in the national Social Forums in Europe tried to advocate for other, marginalized participants, facilitators and dominant elites brushed them off. When individual blacks or queers among USSF organizers complained about racism or homophobia, NGO staffers or other professional activists nodded empathically but did not take action. Only when individuals from these various categories and groups combined forces to form a collective of political translators did they make an impact.

INSTITUTIONALIZING A POSITION FOR CRITICAL POLITICAL TRANSLATORS

I argue here that fully democratic and participatory processes need to institutionalize the practices of political translation. Any disadvantaged community that enters a deliberative process should consider building a collective of political translators. This can be accomplished through strategic outreach to potential intermediaries, groups with standing, and associates who will have the courage, independence, and leverage to intervene disruptively vis-à-vis institutional elites when even the deliberative process begins to be coopted by dominant interests. In Atlanta in the USSF coalition and in Santa Brigida, the disadvantaged selected their own political translators; this can also happen at the international level. Ideally, political translation should be carried out by groups who are both independent from the dominant powers and at least somewhat respected by those powers for the usefulness of their cultural translating work.

Political translation has the potential to reform grassroots democratic practices in a broad arena that includes local and transnational political settings. Activists and theorists alike have suggested the need to develop efficient working practices that enhance the inclusion of democratic voices in discursive and participatory democratic arenas operating at the transnational level. They have, however, neglected the deep problem of positional misunderstandings, at whose center lie not only the structural inequalities of different groups in their capacity to influence political decisions but also a lack of awareness of these inequalities on the part of the dominant elites – a lacuna that political translation is designed to address.

Positional misunderstandings arise amid efforts to address all manner of global collective-action problems, including climate change, poverty, and abandonment of vulnerable populations (Mansbridge 2015). One central theme of this book is that political translators are most useful in solving stalemates in political decision-making regarding questions of redistributive justice and of inequality – where one group takes a public stand of good will and even egalitarian sentiment, and may believe wholeheartedly that this stance is authentic, but in practice is unwilling to listen to another or refuses to share its resources more equally with disadvantaged groups. Given the frequency with which such dynamics arise, political translation could be of use in a nearly infinite variety of contexts where diverse groups of people must find equitable ways of guiding social behavior and sharing resources.

References

Alcalde, Javier. 2015. "Linguistic Justice: An Interdisciplinary Overview of the Literature." *A'dam Multiling Working Paper* #3. http://ssrn.com/abstract=2630104.

———. 2016. "Personality and Subsidiarity: Explaining Linguistic Justice in the Cities." In *Perspectives of Language Communication in the European Union*, edited by Dominika Tekeliová. Nitra (Slovakia): Faculty of Central European Studies, Constantine the Philosopher University. Pp. 35–42.

Andretta, Massimiliano, and Herbert Reiter. 2009. "Parties, Unions, and Movements: The European Left and the ESF." In *Another Europe: Conceptions and Practices of Democracy in the European Social Forums*, edited by Donatella della Porta. New York, NY: Routledge. Pp. 173–203.

Anzaldúa, Gloria. 1999 [1987]. *Borderlands = La frontiera*. San Francisco, CA: Aunt Lute Books.

Apter, Emily. 2006. *The Translation Zone: A New Comparative Literature*. Princeton, NJ: Princeton University Press.

Archibugi, Daniele. 2005. "The Language of Democracy: Vernacular or Esperanto? A Comparison between the Multiculturalist and Cosmopolitan Perspectives." *Political Studies* 53: 537–555.

Arendt, Hannah. 1958. *The Human Condition*, 2nd ed. Chicago, IL: University of Chicago Press.

———. 1969. "On Violence." *New York Review of Books*, February 17.

Baiocchi, Gianpaolo. 2005. *Militants and Citizens: The Politics of Participatory Democracy in Porto Alegre*. Stanford, CA: Stanford University Press.

Baker, Mona. 2016a. "Beyond the Spectacle: Translation and Solidarity in Contemporary Protest Movements." In *Translating Dissent: Voices from and with the Egyptian Revolution*, edited by M. Baker. Abingdon: Routledge. Pp. 1–18.

Berman, Antoine. 2000. "Translation and the Trials of the Foreign." In *The Translation Studies Reader*, edited by Lawrence Venuti. London: Routledge. Pp. 284–298.

Blee, Kathleen. 2012. *Democracy in the Making: How Activist Groups Form*. Oxford: Oxford University Press.

Bob, Clifford. 2005. *The Marketing of Rebellion: Insurgents, Media, and International Activism*. New York, NY: Cambridge University Press.

Boéri, Julie. 2010. "Emerging Narratives of Conference Interpreters' Training: A Case Study of Ad Hoc Training in Babels and the Social Forum." *Peñas* 9: 61–70.

Boéri, Julie, and Stuart Hodkinson. 2004. "Babels and the Politics of Language at the Heart of the Social Forum." *Redpepper* 1(1): no page numbers.

Brewer, Rose M. 2010. "Social Forum Process: The Praxis of Gender, Race, Class, Sexualities." In *Social Change, Resistance and Social Practices*, edited by Richard A. Dello Buono and David Fasenfest. Leiden: Brill. Pp. 57–72.

Butler, Judith, Ernesto Laclau, and Slavoj Zizek. *Contingency, Hegemony, Universality: Contemporary Dialogues on the Left*. London: Verso 2000.

Chabot, Sean. 2007. "Rethinking Nonviolent Action and Contentious Politics: Political Cultures of Nonviolent Opposition in the Indian Independence Movement and Brazil's Landless Workers Movement." *Research in Social Movements, Conflicts, and Change* 27: 91–122.

——— 2012. "Dialogue Matters: Beyond the Transmission Model of transnational Diffusion between Social Movements." In *The Diffusion of Social Movements: Actors, Mechanisms, and Political Effects*, edited by Rebecca Kolins Givan, Kenneth M. Roberts, and Sarah A. Soule. Cambridge: Cambridge University Press. Pp. 99–124.

Chavez, Leo. 2008. *The Latino Threat: Constructing Immigrants, Citizens, and the Nation*. Stanford, CA: Stanford University Press.

Collins, Randall. 2005. *Interaction Ritual Chains*. Princeton, NJ: Princeton University Press.

Conway, Janet. 2011. "Cosmopolitan or Colonial? The World Social Forum as 'Contact Zone'." *Third World Quarterly* 32(2): 217–236.

Crenshaw, Kimberlé Williams. 1989. "Demarginalizing the Intersection of Race and Sex: A Black Feminist Critique of Antidiscrimination Doctrine, Feminist Theory, and Antiracist Politics." *University of Chicago Legal Forum* (1): 139–67.

Deitelhoff, Nicole. 2012. "Leere Versprechungen? Deliberation und Opposition im Kontext transnationaler Legitimitätspolitik." In "Der Aufstieg der Legitimitätspolitik," edited by Anna Geis, Frank Nullmeier, and Christopher Daase, special issue, *Leviathan* 27: 63–82.

Deitelhoff, Nicole, and Thorsten Thiel. 2014. "Keine Widerrede? Opposition und Deliberation in der überstaatlichen Politik." In *Deliberative Demokratie in der Diskussion. Herausforderungen, Bewährungsproben, Kritik*, edited by Anita Landwehr and Rainer Schmalz-Bruns. Baden-Baden: Nomos. Pp. 421–451.

della Porta, Donatella. 2005a. "Making the Polis: Social Forums and Democracy in the Global Justice Movement." *Mobilization* 10(1): 73–94.

——— 2005b. "Multiple Belongings, Tolerant Identities, and the Construction of 'Another Politics': Between the European Social Forum and the Local Social Fora." In *Transnational Protest and Global Activism*, edited by Donatella della Porta and Sidney G. Tarrow. Lanham, MD: Rowman and Littlefield. Pp. 175–202.

——— 2005c. "Deliberation in Movement: Why and How to Study Deliberative Democracy and Social Movements." *Acta Politica* 40(3): 336–350.

——— 2007. "The Global Justice Movement: An Introduction." In *The Global Justice Movement: Cross-national and Transnational Perspectives*, edited by Donatella della Porta. New York, NY: Paradigm. Pp. 1–28.

——— 2009. "Another Europe: An Introduction." In *Another Europe: Conceptions and Practices of Democracy in the European Social Forums*, edited by Donatella della Porta. New York, NY: Routledge. Pp. 3–25.

2012. *Can Democracy Be Saved?* Oxford: Polity.

della Porta, Donatella, Massimiliano Andretta, Lorenzo Mosca, and Herbert Reiter. 2006. *Globalization from Below: Transnational Activists and Protest Networks.* Minneapolis: University of Minnesota Press.

della Porta, Donatella, and Manuela Caiani. 2007. "Europeanization from Below? Social Movements and Europe." *Mobilization* 12(1): 1–20.

2009. *Social Movements and Europeanization.* Oxford: Oxford University Press.

della Porta, Donatella, and Alice Mattoni, eds. 2014. *Spreading Protests: Social Movements in Times of Crisis.* Colchester: ECPR Press.

della Porta, Donatella, and Lorenzo Mosca. 2007. "In Movimento: 'Contamination' in Action and the Italian Global Justice Movement." *Global Networks* 7(1): 1–27.

della Porta, Donatella, and Dieter Rucht, eds. 2009. *Meeting Democracy, Power, and Deliberation in Global Justice Movements.* Cambridge: Cambridge University Press.

Doerr, Nicole. 2007. "Is 'Another' Public Space Actually Possible? Deliberative Democracy and the Case of 'Women Without'." *Journal of International Women's Studies* 8(3): 71–87.

2008. "Deliberative Discussion, Language, and Efficiency in the WSF Process." *Mobilization* 13(4): 395–410.

2009. "Language and Democracy in Movement: Multilingualism and the Case of the European Social Forum Process." *Social Movement Studies* 8(2): 149–165.

2011. "The Disciplining of Dissent and the Role of Empathy in Deliberative Politics: A Ritual Perspective." *Globalizations* 8(4): 519–534.

2012. "Translating Democracy: How Activists in the European Social Forum Practice Multilingual Deliberation." *European Political Science Review* 4(3): 361–384.

Dryzek, Jon. 2009. "Democratization as Deliberative Capacity Building." *Comparative Political Studies* 42: 1379–1402.

Dufour, Pascale. 2010. "The Mobilization against the 2005 Treaty Establishing a Constitution for Europe: A French Mobilization for Another Europe." *Social Movement Studies* 9(4): 425–441.

Eliasoph, Nina. 2011. *Making Volunteers: Civic Life after Welfare's End.* Princeton, NJ: Princeton University Press.

2015. "Spirals of Perpetual Potential: How Empowerment Projects' Noble Missions Tangle in Everyday Interaction." In *Deliberation and Contention: Dilemmas of the New Public Participation,* edited by Caroline Lee, Michael McQuarrie, and Edward T. Walker. Democratizing Inequalities. New York, NY: New York University Press. Pp. 180–201.

Eliasoph, Nina, and Paul Lichterman. 2003. "Culture in Interaction." *American Journal of Sociology* 108(4): 735–794.

European Social Forum/Forum Social Europeen. 2008. "Charter of Principles for Another Europe." www.fse-esf.org/spip.php?article583.

Fantasia, Rick. 2010. "What Happened to the US Left?" *Le Monde Diplomatique,* December 7, 6–7.

Ferree, Myra Marx. 2009. "Inequality, Intersectionality, and the Politics of Discourse: Framing Feminist Alliances." In *The Discursive Politics of Gender Equality: Stretching, Bending, and Policy-Making,* edited by Emanuela Lombardo, Petra Meier, and Mieke Verloo. London: Routledge. Pp. 86–104.

Flesher Fominaya, Cristina. 2015. "Cultural Barriers to Activist Networking: Habitus (In)action in Three European Transnational Encounters." *Antipode* 48(1): 1–21.

Fraser, Nancy. 1992. "Rethinking the Public Sphere: A Contribution to the Critique of Actually Existing Democracy." In *Habermas and the Public Sphere*, edited by Craig Calhoun. Cambridge, MA: MIT Press.

⎯⎯⎯. 2007. "Transnationalizing the Public Sphere: On the Legitimacy and Efficiency of Public Opinion in a Post-Westphalian World." *Theory, Culture, and Society* 24(4): 7–30.

Freeman, Jo. 1972. "The Tyranny of Structurelessness." *The Second Wave* 2(1): 20.

Fung, Archon. 2004. *Empowered Participation: Reinventing Urban Democracy*. Princeton, NJ: Princeton University Press.

Ganz, Marshall, and Emily S. Lin. 2011. "Learning to Lead: A Pedagogy of Practice." In *The Handbook for Teaching Leadership*, edited by Scott Snook, Nitin Nohria, and Rakesh Khurana. Thousand Oaks, CA: SAGE Publications. Pp. 353–366.

Gentzler, Edwin. 2007. *Translation and Identity in the Americas*. London: Routledge.

Ghaziani, Amin. 2008. *The Dividends of Dissent: How Conflict and Culture Work in Lesbian and Gay Marches on Washington*. Chicago, IL: University of Chicago Press.

Gitlin, Todd. 2012. *Occupy Nation: The Roots, the Spirit, and the Promise of Occupy Wall Street*. New York, NY: Harper Collins.

Glaeser, Andreas. 2010. *Political Epistemics: The Secret Police, the Opposition, and the End of East German Socialism*. Chicago, IL: University of Chicago Press.

Glasius, Marlies, and Jill Timms. 2006. "Social Forums: Radical Beacon or Strategic Infrastructure?" In *Global Civil Society Yearbook 5/2005*, edited by Marlies Glasius, Mary Kaldor and Helmut Anheier. Oxford: Oxford University Press. Pp. 175–202.

Goldberg, Harmony, and Rickke Mananzala. 2010. "Right to the City: A Cry and a Demand for a New Urban Struggle." In Karides et al. 2010, 171–180.

Guerrero, Michael Leon. 2008. "The US Social Forum: Building from the Bottom Up." *Society without Borders* 3(1): 168–186.

⎯⎯⎯. 2010. "You Can't Spell Fundraising without F-U-N: The Resource Mob, the Non-Profit Industrial Complex, and the USSF." In Karides et al. 2010, 61–76.

Guttman, Amy, and Dennis Thompson. 1996. *Democracy and Disagreement*. Cambridge: Cambridge University Press.

Habermas, Jürgen. 1984 [1981]. *Theory of Communicative Action*. Vol. 1, *Reason and the Rationalization of Society*. Translated by Thomas A. McCarthy. Boston, MA: Beacon Press.

⎯⎯⎯. 1996. *Between Facts and Norms: Contribution to a Discursive Theory of Law and Democracy*. Cambridge, MA: MIT Press.

Habermas, Jürgen, and Thomas McCarthy. 1977. "Hannah Arendt's Communications Concept of Power." *Social Research* 44(1): 3–24.

Haug, Christoph, Nicolas Haeringer, and Lorenzo Mosca. 2009. "The ESF Organising Process in a Diachronic Perspective." In *Another Europe: Conceptions and Practices of Democracy in the European Social Forums*, edited by Donatella della Porta. New York, NY: Routledge. Pp. 26–45.

Hill Collins, Patricia. 1998. *Fighting Words: Black Women and the Search for Justice*. Minneapolis, MN: University of Minnesota Press.

Inghilleri, Moira. 2012. *Interpreting Justice: Ethics, Politics, and Language*. London: Routledge.

Jasper, James M. 2006. *Getting Your Way: Strategic Dilemmas in the Real World*. Chicago, IL: University of Chicago Press.

Juris, Jeffrey S. 2005. "Social Forums and Their Margins: Networking Logics and the Cultural Politics of Autonomous Space." *Ephemera* 5(2): 253–272.

2008a. *Networking Futures: The Movements against Corporate Globalization*. Durham, NC: Duke University Press.

2008b. "Spaces of Intentionality: Race, Class, and Horizontality at the United States Social Forum" *Mobilization* 13(4): 353–372.

2012. "Reflections on #Occupy Everywhere: Social Media, Public Space, and Emerging Logics of Aggregation." *American Ethnologist* 39(2): 259–279.

2013. "Spaces of Intentionality: Race, Class, and Horizontality at the United States Social Forum." In *Insurgent Encounters: Transnational Activism, Ethnography, and the Political*, edited by Jeffrey J. Juris and Alex Khasnabish. Pp. 39–65.

Juris, Jeffrey S., Erica G. Bushell, Meghan Doran, J. Mathew Judge, Amy Lubitow, Bryan MacCormack, and Christopher Prener. 2014. "Movement Building and the United States Social Forum." *Social Movement Studies* 13(3): 328–348.

Karides, Marina, Walda Katz-Fishman, Rose M. Brewer, Jerome Scott, and Alice Lovelace, eds. 2010. *The United States Social Forum: Perspectives of a Movement*. Chicago, IL: Changemaker.

Klein, Hilary. 2010. "One Movement, Many Languages: Building Multi-lingual Capacity at the US Social Forum." In Karides et al. 2010, 77–88.

Katz-Fishman, Walda, and Jerome Scott. 2010. "Another United States Is Happening: Building Today's Movement from the Bottom-up: The United States Social Forum and Beyond." In Karides et al. 2010, 57–70.

Kitschelt, Herbert. 1993. "Social Movements, Political Parties, and Democratic Theory." *Annals of the American Academy of Political and Social Science* 528: 13–29.

Kymlicka, Will. 2001. *Politics in the Vernacular*. Oxford: Oxford University Press.

Lamont, Michele, and Sada Aksartova. 2002. "Ordinary Cosmopolitanisms: Strategies for Bridging Racial Boundaries among Working-Class Men." *Theory, Culture and Society* 19(4): 1–25.

Lang, Sabine. 2013. *NGOs, Civil Society, and the Public Sphere*. Cambridge: Cambridge University Press.

Lee, Caroline W. 2015. *Do-It-Yourself Democracy: The Rise of the Public Engagement Industry*. Oxford University Press.

Lee, Caroline W., Michael McQuarrie, and Edward T. Walker. 2015. "Rising Participation and Declining Democracy." In *Democratizing Inequalities: Dilemmas of the New Public Participation*, edited by Caroline W. Lee, Michael McQuarrie, and Edward T. Walker. New York, NY: New York University Press. Pp. 3–26.

Leondar-Wright, Betsy. 2014. *Missing Class: Strengthening Social Movement Groups by Seeing Class Cultures*. Ithaca, NY: Cornell University Press.

Lépinard, Éléonore. 2014. "Doing Intersectionality: Repertoires of Feminist Practices in France and Canada." *Gender and Society* 28(6): 877–903.

Levitt, Peggy, and Sally E. Merry. 2007. "Vernacularization on the Ground: Local Uses of Global Women's Rights in Peru, China, India, and the United States." *Global Networks* 9(4): 441–461.

Lichterman, Paul. 1996. *The Search for Political Community: American Activists Reinventing Commitment*. New York, NY: Cambridge University Press.

Mansbridge, Jane. 1983. *Beyond Adversary Democracy*. Chicago, IL: Chicago University Press.

2003. "Rethinking Representation." *American Political Science Review* (97)4: 515–528.

2015. "Resisting Resistance." In *Transformations of Democracy: Crisis, Protest, and Legitimation*, edited by Robin Celikates, Regina Kreide, and Tilo Wesche. New York, NY: Routledge. Pp. 140–157.

Maeckelbergh, Marianne. 2004. "Perhaps We Should Just Flip a Coin: Macro and Microstructures of the European Social Forum Processes." In *Euromovements Newsletter* #1, edited by Oscar Reyes, Hilary Wainwright, Mayo Fuster i Morell, and Marco Berlinguer, December. www.euromovements.info/newsletter/flipacoin.htm.

2009. *The Will of the Many: How the Alterglobalisation Movement Is Changing the Face of Democracy*. London: Pluto.

Mattoni, Alice. 2012. *Media Practices and Protest Politics: How Precarious Workers Mobilise*. London: Routledge.

Mayer, Margit. 2009a. "The 'Right to the City' in the Context of Shifting Mottos of Urban Social Movements." In "Cities for People, Not for Profit," special issue, *City: Analysis of Urban Trends, Culture, Theory, Policy, Action* 13(2–3): 362–374.

2009b. "Social Cohesion and Anti-poverty Policies in US Cities." In *Social Cohesion in Europe and the Americas/Cohesión social en Europa y las Américas*, edited by Harlan Koff. Bern: Peter Lang. Pp. 311–334.

2012. "Crisis City: Die Krise der amerikanischen Stadt" [Crisis City: The Crisis of the American City]. In *Medien, Macht und Metropolen*, edited by Marco Althaus, Gerhard Göhler, Cornelia Schmalz-Jacobsen, and Christian Walther. Frankfurt.: Peter Lang. Pp. 67–82.

2013. "First World Urban Activism: Beyond Austerity Urbanism and Creative City Politics." *City: Analysis of Urban Trends, Culture, Theory, Policy, Action* 17(2): 5–19.

McAdam, Doug, and Karina Kloos, 2014. *Deeply Divided: Racial Politics and Social Movements in Postwar America*. Oxford: Oxford University Press.

McQuarrie, Michael. 2015. "No Contest: Participatory Technologies and the Transformation of Urban Authority." In *Deliberation and Contention: Dilemmas of the New Public Participation*, edited by Caroline Lee, Michael McQuarrie, and Edward T. Walker. Democratizing Inequalities. New York, NY: New York University Press. Pp. 83–101.

Meyer, David S. 2007. *The Politics of Protest: Social Movements in America*. New York, NY: Oxford University Press.

Meyer, David S., and Amanda Pullum. 2015. "The Social Movement Society, the Tea Party, and the Democratic Deficit." In *Deliberation and Contention. Dilemmas of the New Public Participation*, edited by Caroline Lee, Michael McQuarrie, and Edward T. Walker. Democratizing Inequalities. New York, NY: New York University Press. Pp. 219–236.

Mezzadra, Sandro, 2007. "Living in Transition: Toward a Heterolingual Theory of the Multitude." *Transversal* 6: no page numbers.

Minkoff, Debra C., and Jon Agnone. 2010. "Consolidating Social Change: The Consequences of Foundation Funding for Developing Movement Infrastructures." In *American Foundations: Roles and Contributions, Contributions of Foundations*, edited by Helmut Anheier and David Hammack. Washington, DC: Brookings Institution Press. Pp. 347–367.

Mische, Ann. 2008. *Partisan Publics: Communication and Contention across Brazilian Youth Activist Networks*. Princeton, NJ: Princeton University Press.

Mokre, Monika. 2015. *Solidarität als Übersetzung—Überlegungen zum Refugee Protest Camp Vienna*. Edited by Andrea Hummer. Vienna: Transversal.

Mosca, Lorenzo. 2007. "Fra leadership e decisione: Il dilemma della rappresentanza nelle aree di movimento." In *Partecipazione e rappresentanza nelle mobilitazioni locali*, edited by Tommaso Vitale. Milan: Franco Angeli.

Nanz, Patrizia. 2006. *Europolis: Constitutional Patriotism beyond the Nation State*. Manchester: Manchester University Press.

2009. "Mobility, Migrants, and Solidarity: Towards an Emerging European Citizenship Regime." In *Migration and Mobilities: Citizenship, Borders, and Gender*, edited by Seyla Benhabib and Judith Resnik. New York, NY: New York University Press. Pp. 410–438.

Nanz, Patrizia, and Jens Steffek. 2004. "Global Governance, Participation, and the Public Sphere." *Government and Opposition* 39(2): 314–335.

Nicholls Walter, J., and Justus Uitermark. 2016. *Cities and Social Movements: Immigrant Rights Activism in the United States, France, and the Netherlands, 1970–2015*. London: Wiley Blackwell.

Nuñes, Rodrigo. 2005. "Networks, Open Spaces, Horizontality: Instantiations." *Ephemera* 5(2): 297–318.

Olick, J. K., and D. Levy. 1998. "Collective Memory and Cultural Constraint: Holocaust Myth and Rationality in German Politics." *American Sociological Review* 62: 920–936.

Phillips, Anne. 1993. *Democracy and Difference*. Cambridge: Polity Press.

2007. *Multiculturalism without Culture*. Princeton, NJ: Princeton University Press.

Pleyers, Geoffrey. 2010. *Alter-globalization: Becoming Actors in a Global Age*. London: Polity.

Plotke, David. 1997. "Representation Is Democracy." *Constellations* 4: 19–34.

Polletta, Francesca. 2002. *Freedom Is an Endless Meeting: Democracy in American Social Movements*. Chicago, IL: Chicago University Press.

2006. *It Was Like a Fever: Storytelling in Protest and Politics*. Chicago, IL: Chicago University Press.

Polletta, Francesca. 2008. "Culture and Social Movements." *Annals of the American Academy of Political and Social Science* 619: 1.

2015. "Public Deliberation and Political Contention." In *Deliberation and Contention. Dilemmas of the New Public Participation*, edited by Caroline Lee, Michael McQuarrie, and Edward T. Walker. Democratizing Inequalities. New York, NY: New York University Press. Pp. 222–247.

Ponniah, Thomas. 2008. "The Meaning of the US Social Forum." *Societies without Borders* 3(1): 187–195.

Poo, Ai-jen, Andrea Cristina Mercado, Jill Shenker, Xiomara Corpeño, and Allison Julien. 2010. "National Domestic Workers Alliance." In Karides et al. 2010, 155–169.

Reyes, Oscar. 2006. "Exception or Rule? The Case of the London ESF 2004." In Marlies Glasius, Mary Kaldor, and Helmut Anheier (eds.), *Global Civil Society 2005/6*. London: Sage. Pp. 243–244.

Rancière, Jacques. 1995. *La Mésentente: Politique et philosophie*. Paris: Galilée.

Risse, Thomas. 2000. "'Let's Argue!' Communicative Action in International Relations." *International Organization* 54(1): 1–39.

Robnett, Belinda. 1997. *How Long? How Long?: African American Women in the Struggle for Civil Rights*: Oxford: Oxford University Press.

Rootes, Christopher, and Clare Saunders. 2007. The Global Justice Movement in Great Britain. In *The Global Justice Movement: Cross-national and Transnational Perspectives*, edited by Donatella della Porta and Massimiliano Andretta. Boulder, CO: Paradigm. Pp. 128–156.

Roth, Silke. 2003. *Building Movement Bridges: The Coalition of Labor Union Women*. Westport, CT: Praeger.

Rucht, Dieter. 2002. "The EU as a Target of Political Mobilisation: Is There a Europeanisation of Conflict?" In *L'action collective en Europe/Collective Action in Europe*, edited by Richard Balme, Didier Chabanet, and Vincent Wright. Paris: Presses de Sciences Po. Pp. 163–194.

2009. "Types and Patterns of Intragroup Controversies." In *Meeting Democracy, Power, and Deliberation in Global Justice Movements*. Cambridge: Cambridge University Press. 48–71.

Rucht, Dieter, Simon Teune, and Mundo Yang. 2007. "Moving Together: Global Justice Movements in Germany." In *The Global Justice Movement: Cross-national and Transnational Perspectives*, edited by Donatella della Porta and Massimiliano Andretta. New York, NY: Paradigm. Pp. 157–183.

Sakai, Naoki. 1997. *Translation and Subjectivity: On "Japan" and Cultural Nationalism*, Minneapolis, MN: University of Minnesota Press.

Sanford, Victoria. 2003. *Buried Secrets: Truth and Human Rights in Guatemala*. New York, NY: Palgrave Macmillan.

Santos, Boaventura de Sousa. 2006. *The Rise of the Global Left*. London: Zed Press.

Schneider, Nathan. 2013. *Thank You, Anarchy: Notes from the Occupy Apocalypse*. Berkeley: University of California Press.

Schönleitner, Günter. 2003. "World Social Forum: Making Another World Possible?" In *Globalizing Civic Engagement: Civil Society and Transnational Action*, edited by John Clark. London: Earthscan. Pp. 127–149.

Schwab, Gabriele. 2010. *Haunting Legacies: Violent Histories and Transgenerational Trauma*. New York, NY: Columbia University Press.

Sintomer, Yves, Anja Röcke, and Carsten Herzberg. 2016. *Participatory Budgeting in Europe: Participatory Democracy and Public Governance*. London: Routledge.

Sitrin, Marina, and Dario Azzellini. 2014. *They Can't Represent Us!: Reinventing Democracy from Greece to Occupy*. New York, NY: Verso.

Smith, Jackie. 2005. "Building Bridges or Building Walls? Explaining Regionalization among Transnational Social Movement Organizations" *Mobilization* 10(2): 251–269.

2007. *Social Movements for Global Democracy*. Baltimore, MD: Johns Hopkins University Press.

2010. "Globalization and Strategic Peacebuilding." In *Strategies of Peace: Transforming Conflict in a Violent World*, edited by D. Philpott and G. F. Powers. New York, NY: Oxford University Press. Pp. 247–270.

2012. "Connecting Social Movements and Political Moments: Bringing Movement—Building Tools from Global Justice to Occupy Wall Street Activism" *Interface* 4(2): 369–382.

2017. "Inclusive Placemaking: Localizing Human Rights in Response to Global Urban Crises and Right-Wing Populism." Paper prepared for the ASA in Montreal.

Smith, Jackie, Scott Byrd, Ellen Reese, and Elizabeth Smythe, eds. 2012. *A Handbook of World Social Forum Activism*. Boulder, CO: Paradigm.

Smith, Jackie, Jeffrey S. Juris, and the USSF Research Collective. 2008. "We Are the Ones We Have Been Waiting For: The US Social Forum in Context" *Mobilization* 13(4): 373–394.

Smith, Jackie, Marina Karides, Marc Becker, Dorval Brunelle, Christopher Chase-Dunn, Donatella della Porta, Rosalba Icaza, Jeffrey Juris, Lorenzo Mosca, Ellen Reese, Peter (Jay) Smith, and Rolando Vasquez. 2007. *Global Democracy and the World Social Forums*. Boulder, CO: Paradigm.

Smith, Jackie, and Dawn Wiest. 2012. *Social Movements in the World-System: The Politics of Crisis and Transformation*. New York, NY: Russell Sage Foundation.

Smith, William. 2004. "Democracy, Deliberation, and Disobedience." *Res Publica* 10: 353–377.

Snyder, Anna. 2006. "Fostering Transnational Dialogue: Lessons Learned from Women Peace Activists." *Globalizations* 3: 31–47.

Strolovitch, Dara Z. 2007. *Affirmative Advocacy: Race, Class, and Gender in Interest Group Politics*. Chicago, IL: University of Chicago Press.

Tallise, Robert B. 2001. "Deliberativist Responses to Activist Challenges: A Continuation of Young's Dialectic." *Philosophy and Social Criticism* 31(4): 423–444.

Talpin, Julien. 2006. "Who Governs in Participatory Governance Institutions? The Impact of Citizen Participation in Municipal Decision-Making Processes in a Comparative Perspective." In *Towards DIY-Politics. Participatory and Direct Democracy at the Local Level in Europe*, edited by Pascal Dewitt, Emmanuel-Benoit Pilet, Hervig Reynaert, and Kristoph Steyvers. Bruges: Vanden Broele. Pp. 103–125.

Tarrow, Sidney. 2006. *The New Transnational Activism*. Cambridge: Cambridge University Press.

Taylor, Charles. 1995. *Philosophical Arguments*. Cambridge, MA: Harvard University Press.

Teivainen, Teivo. 2002. "The World Social Form and Global Democratisation: Learning from Porto Alegre." *Third World Quarterly* 23(4): 621–632.

Thompson, Dennis F. 2008. "Deliberative Democratic Theory and Empirical Political Science." *Annual Review of Political Science* 11: 497–520.

Tijerina, Roberto. 2009. "What Did They Say? Interpreting for Social Justice: An Introductory Curriculum." Highlander Research and Education Center, Fall. www.intergroupresources.com/rc/Highlander%20curric.pdf.

Tymoczko, Maria. 1999. *Translation in a Postcolonial Context*. Manchester: St. Jerome Publishing.

Tymoczko, Maria. 2007. *Enlarging Translation, Empowering Translators*. Manchester: St. Jerome Publishing.

Tymoczko, Maria, and Edwin Gentzler, eds. 2002. *Translation and Power*. Amherst, MA: University of Massachusetts Press.

Urbinati, Nadia. 2000. "Representation as Advocacy: A Study of Democratic Deliberation." *Political Theory* 28(6): 758–786.

Urbinati, Nadia, and Marc E. Warren. 2008. "The Concept of Representation in Contemporary Democratic Theory." *Annual Review of Political Science* 11: 387–412.

USSF Research Collective. 2010. "What Happens at the US Social Forum." www .ussocialforum.net.

Van Parijs, Philippe. 2011. *Linguistic Justice for Europe and for the World*. New York, NY: Oxford University Press.

Venuti, Laurence. 1992. *Rethinking Translation: Discourse, Subjectivity, Ideology*. London: Routledge.

Vintagen, Stellan. 2015. *A Theory of Nonviolent Action: How Civil Resistance Works*. London: ZED Books.

Wagner-Pacifici, Robin. 2005. *The Art of Surrender: Decomposing Sovereignty at Conflict's End*. Chicago, IL: University of Chicago Press.

Waterman, Peter. 2004. "The World Social Forum and the Global Justice and Solidarity Movement: A Backgrounder." In *The World Social Forum: Challenging Empires*, edited by Jai Sen, Anita Anand, Arturo Escobar, and Peter Waterman. New Delhi: The Viveka Foundation. Pp. 55–66.

Whitaker, Chico. 2004. "The WSF as an Open Space." In *The World Social Forum: Challenging Empires*, edited by Jai Sen, Anita Anand, Arturo Escobar, and Peter Waterman. New Delhi: The Viveka Foundation. Pp. 111–121.

Whittier, Nancy. 1995. *Feminist Generations: The Persistence of the Radical Women's Movement*. Philadelphia, PA: Temple University Press.

2014. "Rethinking Coalitions: Anti-pornography Feminists, Conservatives, and Relationships between Collaborative Adversarial Movements." *Social Problems* 61 (2): 175–193.

Wodak, Ruth. 1998. *Disorders of Discourse*. London: Longman.

2015. *The Politics of Fear: What Right-Wing Populist Discourses Mean*. London: Sage.

Wood, Lesley J. 2005. "Bridging the Chasms: The Case of People's Global Action." In *Coalitions across Borders: Transnational Protest and the Neoliberal Order*, edited by Joe Bandy and Jackie Smith. Lanham, MD: Rowman and Littlefield. Pp. 95–119.

2012. *Direct Action, Deliberation, and Diffusion: Collective Action after the WTO Protests in Seattle*. Cambridge Studies in Contentious Politics. Cambridge: Cambridge University Press.

World Social Forum Organizing Committee. 2001. *World Social Forum Charter of Principles*. Porto Alegre. www.fse-esf.org/spip.php?article586.

Wainwright, Hilary. 2006. "Imagine There's No Leaders." Transnational Institute. www.tni.org/es/node/14242.

Wodak, Ruth. 1996. *Disorders of Discourse*. London: Longman.

2015. *The Politics of Fear: What Right-Wing Populist Discourses Mean*. London: SAGE Publications.

Young, Iris M. 1996. "Communication and the Other: Beyond Deliberative Democracy." In *Democracy and Difference: Contesting the Boundaries of the Political*, edited by Seyla Benhabib. Princeton, NJ: Princeton University Press. Pp. 120–136.

1998. "Difference as a Resource for Democratic Communication." In *Deliberative Democracy*, edited by James Bohman and William Rehg. Cambridge, MA: MIT Press. Pp. 383–407.

2000. *Inclusion and Democracy*. New York, NY: Oxford University Press.

2003. "Activist Challenges to Deliberative Democracy." In *Debating Deliberative Democracy*, edited by James S. Fishkin and Peter Laslett. Malden, MA: Blackwell. Pp. 102–120.

Yuval-Davis, Nira. 2006. "Intersectionality and Feminist Politics." *European Journal of Women's Studies* 13(3): 193–209.

Zepeda-Millán, Chris. 2016. "Weapons of the (Not So) Weak: Immigrant Mass Mobilization in the US South." *Critical Sociology* 42(2): 269–287.

Index

Books in the Series (continued from p. ii)

Charles Tilly, *The Politics of Collective Violence*

Marisa von Bülow, *Building Transnational Networks: Civil Society and the Politics of Trade in the Americas*

Lesley J. Wood, *Direct Action, Deliberation, and Diffusion: Collective Action after the WTO Protests in Seattle*

Stuart A. Wright, *Patriots, Politics, and the Oklahoma City Bombing*

Deborah Yashar, *Contesting Citizenship in Latin America: The Rise of Indigenous Movements and the Postliberal Challenge*

Andrew Yeo, *Activists, Alliances, and Anti-U.S. Base Protests*